Dear Steve,

From one Clearview boy to another, I had to send you a copy of my book since you're in it!

Say hello to your parents for me.

All the best,

Alan

Misdiagnosis

A Physician's Triumph Over His Thirty-Year Battle With Depression

By Alan R. Cohen, M.D.

Misdiagnosis *is a memoir. All the events described in this book are true; however, certain names have been changed to protect the privacy of these individuals.*

ISBN 0-7414-3646-9

Published by:

INFINITY
PUBLISHING.COM

1094 New DeHaven Street, Suite 100
West Conshohocken, PA 19428-2713
Info@buybooksontheweb.com
www.buybooksontheweb.com
Toll-free (877) BUY BOOK
Local Phone (610) 941-9999
Fax (610) 941-9959

Printed in the United States of America

Printed on Recycled Paper

Published March 2007

Acknowledgments

There have been many people who have helped me along my path. I wish to extend a special thanks to Trudy Griswold and Dr. Akhter Ahsen for their words of wisdom and kind support and to my editors for their help and guidance. I want to express my love and gratitude to my friends, Anthony Bove and Jimmy Mancini, who have been my pillars of strength, to my sister, Kathi Fredericks, who has always been there for me, and to my daughter, Staci, whose decision to be part of my life again has been more healing for me than words can ever say. Most importantly, I want to thank my wife, Bobbie, whose unconditional love, devotion and unrelenting belief in me made this all possible.

Preface

As a physician who battled depression for over thirty years, I had the rare perspective of having been both one of the 100 million people worldwide who suffer from this debilitating and sometimes fatal illness, and one who sought to alleviate the suffering of others who were also burdened by this problem. Depression is a global epidemic; this illness is the world's leading cause of disability. In the year 2000 alone, a million people throughout the world committed suicide, a disturbing figure, equal to the combined number of deaths from war and homicide. Many of these people could have been helped if they had been diagnosed correctly with ***Bipolar 2 Disorder***, instead of major, or "unipolar," depression, and had received the appropriate treatment.

Misdiagnosis of this illness can sometimes mean the difference between life and death since the lifetime risk of suicide and functional impairment is substantially greater in bipolar disorders than in major depression. The misdiagnosis of this mood disorder had devastating consequences for me. One purpose of this book is to increase awareness of this little-known psychiatric disorder so that people who suffer from this problem can receive the early intervention that will allow them to avoid the suffering that I have endured during my life.

My first suicide attempt occurred when I was twenty years old. At that time, I was diagnosed and treated for major depression with antidepressants. Despite treatment with a variety of these medications, in the years that followed I tried to take my life on numerous occasions. These recurrent episodes of severe depression during the course of my life led to twelve psychiatric hospitalizations and over thirty electroshock therapy treatments. A major turning point in my life, which started me on my path to wellness, occurred in 2004 when my long standing diagnosis of major depression was changed to Bipolar 2 Disorder.

Various issues converged throughout my life to trigger my many encounters with depression. In July of 1999, I endured the pain of losing my dad. I was diagnosed with kidney cancer two months later, initiating a battle with this illness that took a significant toll on my physical, emotional, and mental health. Following that, I had emergency surgery for a lung abscess caused by an injury sustained when I overdosed on medication during one of my bouts of depression. Less than a year later, I lost my mother to metastatic lung cancer. All of these stresses combined to drain my emotional reserves.

There were major stressors in my professional life as well. In my twenty years as a physician who practiced alternative medicine, I had to endure the scrutiny of a medical community all too often critical of this new paradigm of healing. From 1996-2000, I was forced to engage in a legal battle with the Connecticut Medical Board that was due in part to my beliefs and principles in the practice of alternative medicine. In March of 2000, I was named, along with other physicians and chiropractors, in a $60 million racketeering lawsuit that landed my picture on the front pages of the *New York Post*. These issues were eventually settled, but the financial, physical, emotional, and mental stress from this legal quagmire triggered another episode of suicidal depression.

There was also a deep psychological wound that made me vulnerable to this illness. I had an emotionally distant, demanding mother who was impossible to please no matter how hard I tried. She also had been psychologically scarred at the age of sixteen when her mother committed suicide. In order to seal off this painful memory, she had built a wall around her heart, a wall that also sealed off her ability to freely give and receive love. My self-esteem and sense of self-worth suffered tremendously as a result of this relationship. A major factor that also started me on my road to recovery occurred when I received the therapy that helped me heal this psychic wound.

In order to understand Bipolar 2 Disorder, it is important to make absolutely clear the difference between the bipolar disorders and major depression. ***Bipolar 1 Disorder***, previously known as manic-depression, is characterized by both a manic phase and a depressed phase that mirrors the clinical picture of major depression. Symptoms commonly seen in the manic phase of bipolar 1 include increased energy, euphoria, racing thoughts, rapid speech, irritability, need of little sleep, poor judgment, impulsivity, increased sex drive, and psychosis. Bipolar 2 Disorder, on the other hand, is associated with a "hypomanic" phase in which there is no psychosis and the manic symptoms are subtler and not as overt as in bipolar 1. But like bipolar 1, this mood disorder also has a depressive phase that mirrors the symptoms of major depression, the latter not being associated with any manic or hypomanic symptoms.

Studies have shown that as many as 40 percent of both inpatients and outpatients diagnosed with depression are subsequently found to have one of these two bipolar disorders, which, although previously believed to affect two million Americans, actually affects closer to ten million. Patients like me who are suffering from Bipolar 2 Disorder, are more frequently misdiagnosed with major depression than those with bipolar 1 for primarily two reasons. First, patients feel remarkably well when hypomanic and are thus unlikely to spontaneously report these episodes. Second, they do not display the psychotic symptoms associated with the mania of bipolar 1, symptoms that are much easier to recognize and diagnose.

In my case, after each depressive episode, I was filled with intoxicating joy and happiness that I considered to be a sign of a normal return to health, particularly since these feelings only enhanced my enjoyment of life. Also, with no symptoms of psychosis, I was able to fly under the radar screen of clinical detection for years and not be diagnosed with this disorder until much later in life.

A thorough case history as well as knowledge of this illness by the physician is essential in making the diagnosis of Bipolar 2 Disorder because the treatment of bipolar disorders and major depression are distinctly different. The antidepressants used to treat major depression are usually ineffective in the treatment of bipolar disorders. In addition, some studies suggest that antidepressants can actually trigger mania and worsen the course of this disease. In my case, although I had been prescribed a wide variety of these medications over time, my episodes of depression only increased in frequency and severity. A different class of drugs, known as ***mood stabilizers***, is the treatment of choice for bipolar disorders.

Although I believe that medication can be important in the treatment of mental illness, in my experience from years of practice in the field of alternative medicine, I will also share case histories of patients with depression who had underlying diseases that were either ignored or not recognized by the medical profession. When these illnesses were diagnosed and treated, symptoms of depression improved dramatically without the use of medication.

Another aim in writing this book is to discuss the many modalities that helped guide me out of the maze of depression. Such modalities included a cutting-edge form of psychotherapy known as ***eidetic imagery***. I also applied my knowledge of the various healing arts available in the field of alternative medicine such as homeopathy, acupuncture, Bach flower remedies, aromatherapy, and foot reflexology. Equally important in my healing were the lessons I learned along my spiritual journey. It is my sincere hope that all of this information will also aid people who suffer from this illness.

Chapter One

Peering down from the nineteenth floor of the dormitory tower, I squeezed through the window and prepared for my departure from this life. As I started to make the leap that would finally put an end to my suffering, a voice called out to me, "Alan! DON'T!!!" It was the therapist who had been counseling me during my first episode of depression. I turned to him with a sigh of disappointment tinged with relief and grabbed his outstretched hand, which guided me to safety. Soon, I was on the road to what would be the first of many psychiatric hospitalizations that would span the next thirty years of my life.

This first encounter with depression occurred in 1973 during my third year of college at SUNY at Albany, when I was twenty. The most immediate factor that led me down the path of despair, despondency, and desperation that ultimately culminated in an attempt to take my life had to do with the relationship with my girlfriend. Living away from home for the first time was a struggle. In my first year of college, I rushed into this relationship subconsciously seeking the comfort and support that I had grown accustomed to while living with my family. She became the center of my life. Two years later, when the love that I had for her faded, my life began to unravel.

Looking back now, there were signs in my childhood that pointed to the long road of depression that I would travel down in the years that lay ahead. Growing up, I lived with my mother, Dorothy; my father, Eddie; and my younger sister, Kathi, in a small but cozy two-bedroom garden apartment complex in Bayside, Queens. My sister and I shared one bedroom, until puberty hit. This already small room was then divided in half, separated by Sheetrock and a sliding door. Even though my new room was barely big enough to fit my bed, my desk, and me, what mattered most was that it was *my* room! Despite the fact that the four of us shared tight quarters, not to mention having to share a bathroom with two females, I never felt crowded or cramped in this apartment. It always felt like "home."

This garden apartment complex was one of several such developments that sprang up in the late 1940s, offering relatively inexpensive but aesthetically appealing housing to World War II veterans. This sprawling complex consisted of two-story brick buildings that were grouped together in a U shape design called "courts." It was a tightly knit community with all the adults being close in age, sharing similar backgrounds and all having children who were about my age. So, I was never short on friends.

We modeled our games based on the architectural designs offered to us by our neighborhood. Each apartment had a stoop, so we played stoopball. There was also a sidewalk lining the inner perimeter of the court that was neatly divided into symmetrical boxes. From that design, we created such games as "box baseball" and "five boxes."

The biggest debate among my friends, for those old enough to remember, was which ball was the best to use for which games: Pense Pinky or Spalding. For box baseball, I preferred the Spalding because its softer consistency allowed me to put a greater backspin on my pitch, making me almost unbeatable. For the other games, where greater bounce and distance were the main criteria, the Pense Pinky was far superior.

In what we called "the back," where the garages and parking lot were located, we played two variations of stickball: "hitting out" and "pitching in." Each had its own rules and skills, but they did share some features. These games were an important part of the fun-filled summer afternoons of my youth.

There is a painful memory from my early adolescent

years, however, that influenced my self-esteem for many years to come. As puberty struck and the surging of hormones caused all of my friends to gain many inches in height and sprout hair over various parts of their anatomy almost overnight, I remained stuck in my pre-pubertal body, hairless except for my head and barely reaching five feet in height. As they all joked about having wet dreams, I laughed along with them, wanting to be one of the boys but not understanding why they would be bragging about bladder problems. I was very self-conscious about my lack of development and one incident poured salt on this open wound.

I was walking with my friend Steve, who was my age but towered over me. We met another friend, one year our senior, who asked me, in a voice tinged with biting sarcasm and disdain, when I was going to "get some height." This passing remark wounded me deeply, and even when I reached my adult height of close to six feet, I was still predisposed to perceive myself in the years that followed as a ninety-eight-pound weakling.

I have many warm memories of life with my family. My dad was a kind, loving man. To paraphrase Will Rogers, I never met anyone who didn't like him. His heart's greatest desire was to make sure that his family was happy. He had thick, curly, black hair; dark eyes; and a quick, easy smile framed by deep dimples. I still remember Dad's contagious, high-pitched, staccato laugh that was often ignited by watching a Peter Sellers movie. It would spread like wildfire throughout our small apartment, causing all of us to double over in uncontrollable spasms of laughter.

His other great love, second only to his family, was the Brooklyn Dodgers. He literally became sick whenever they lost a game, avoiding all newspapers and radio and television sport shows that reminded him of this tragic event. He never forgave the Dodgers when they moved to Los Angeles. Dad then became a devoted New York Mets fan and because I was devoted to my father, they also became my team.

My father graduated from high school. However, the

academic world was not his strong point. Dad explored various avenues to earn a living and provide for his family. He first tried his hand at beautician school, but he quickly lost interest in that line of work. After that, he became a taxi cab driver, but that didn't suit him either. Then he pursued one of the oldest Jewish traditions, dating back centuries; he became a "peddler." Dad purchased a "route" that consisted of a list of customers who lived in the tenements of Brooklyn neighborhoods such as Bedford-Stuyvesant and Ocean Hill Brownsville.

Many of my father's clients were on welfare and, consequently, did not have either have enough cash or good enough credit to buy household appliances and furniture. As a consequence, Dad became their "credit card," taking them to the various merchants that he knew in the area to purchase their TVs and other items for which they in turn would pay him back with interest on a monthly basis. Whenever my friends asked me what my father did for a living, I would scratch my head, trying to find a way to condense his job description into three words or less. I finally asked my father to sum it up for me. "Tell them that I am a credit installment salesman," he said. Sounded good to me.

However, this job had the potential of being hazardous since it involved going into what were then the ghettos of Brooklyn, carrying a good amount of cash. I am certain, as I look back at it now, that the stress from having to deal with some clients who tried to renege on their debt and the fact that he was mugged twice contributed to his poor health, culminating in an ulcer and many heart attacks.

The highlight of my summer vacation was spending the day with my dad on his route. My father was an expert in knowing the best places to park so that he could make a quick entrance and exit from the buildings where his customers lived. I remember running breathlessly behind him, trying to keep up as he sprinted up the steps of one apartment building after another. I also observed firsthand how he used his charm and humor to put his customers at ease and how they in turn treated him with affection and respect.

My mother and her sister Mary, who was my favorite aunt, also worked in the area as bookkeepers. The best part of the day was joining them for lunch in the finest Italian deli in town: Benny's. I can still taste those meatball heroes. And since good food was important to both of us, we made frequent trips to nearby Chinatown and sat double-parked in front of Dad's favorite restaurant, eating the best lo mein known to mankind.

My father was a very funny man in his own way. Dad always boasted that he never forgot a face. He was right. The only problem was that he never remembered the name of the person attached to that face, so he improvised. A good example of this was the time he was struggling to remember the name of the folk group, Peter, Paul, and Mary. Try as he might, the names wouldn't come, so he blurted out, "I remember now: Sol, Mary, and Becky." With tears of laughter streaming down my cheeks I said to him, "Not bad Dad, one out of three. You're getting better!"

Dad had the patience of a Buddha when it came to his children and grandchildren. When I was living at home in New York, he drove me to a hotel in New Jersey where I took the exam for my family practice boards. I was there for eight hours and the whole time he sat peacefully in the lobby, reading the paper and people watching. After the exam was over he told me, with a big smile on his face, that he saw a basketball player from his favorite team, the New York Knicks. That was enough to make his day.

My father taught me many things as I was growing up, but the one lesson that stands out in my mind is what I learned from him about the value of honesty. As a young boy, I got into mischief from time to time, like most boys do. Whenever Dad found out what trouble I had gotten into, he would say to me, "Alan, I am upset with what you have done, but I would be more upset if you lied to me. Please, don't ever lie to me." My father's integrity and honesty are two of the most important traits that I inherited from this wonderful man.

My mom, though petite, radiated strength, poise, and confidence. Even in my later years when I was a full foot taller than her, she seemed to loom over me. Once, as I went to hug her, I looked down and said in disbelief, "Mom, have you always been this short?" She was "the brains" of the family. Although never accomplishing her dream of going to college, she satisfied her thirst for knowledge and intellectual stimulation by becoming an avid reader and taking adult education courses in such subjects as Jewish literature, film making, and her favorite subject, Yiddish.

Through her readings and research, Mom became a self-proclaimed *maven*, which is a Yiddish term for expert, in many fields. I was often amazed that with only a high school education, she had accumulated such a vast array of esoteric knowledge that she was able to meet what I considered to be one of the most daunting academic challenges in the world: completing the crossword puzzle in every Sunday edition of the *New York Times.* Mom was impressive.

She also became an authority in the field of medicine. Although I had gone through four years of medical school and three years of a family practice residency, Mom always thought that she knew more about medicine in general than I did. She did, however, have one humbling experience that put in her place in regard to her medical expertise.

When my Uncle Larry, her brother, had just had a heart attack, Mom asked the cardiologist if her brother was "fibrillating," a technical medical term for the very erratic heartbeat that can occur as a consequence of a heart attack. Assuming that she was a doctor, he bombarded her with complex medical lingo until finally she was forced to admit that, in the field of medicine, she was just a "wannabe."

My mother did teach me a lot about music as I was growing up. Just as I became an ardent Mets fan because of my father's love for that team, Mom's devotion to her favorite singers including Frank Sinatra, Tony Bennett, and Billie Holiday, also made me a lifelong fan of these talented vocalists. Every Sunday morning she listened to her favorite deejay, Jonathan Schwartz. I often joined her in a sing-along as he played selections from his vast collection of recordings by these artists.

She was definitely the "go-to" parent whenever I was having any problem with my school work. While I inherited my mother's trait of pursuing knowledge and academic excellence, my younger sister inherited my father's gift of social graces, but along with that, his weaker academic skills. My sister and I went to the same school and had the same teachers, although she was two years behind me. I was the trailblazer, excelling in all of my classes. Unfortunately, Kathi had the burden of trying to follow in my footsteps, never living up to our mother's or her teachers' expectations. Mom's constant criticism of Kathi for her poor academic performance wounded my sister deeply and produced emotional scars that she carries to this day.

My mother was a tough person to love. When she was sixteen, her mother committed suicide. Mom never spoke of this tragedy. Her silence on this matter I believe was an attempt to seal off this agonizing memory. In doing so, she had built a wall around her heart, a wall that also unfortunately blocked her ability to freely receive and give love to those closest to her – me, Kathi and Dad. On those rare occasions when she did let down her guard, I was able to enter her heart, only to be ejected the moment that I said or did something that did not meet her approval. She attempted to bury her pain, hoping that it would go away if she ignored it. But instead, it festered and made her bitter. Often, I would be the target of one of her vitriolic outbursts and was snared on her barbs of criticism and sarcasm. Despite all this, I loved her and I knew that she loved me.

I grew up in a predominantly Jewish neighborhood, fully immersed in the traditions and beliefs of the Jewish culture, including such customary rites of passage as going to Hebrew school and proudly singing my *Haftorah* at my *Bar Mitzvah*, although with no idea of what the words meant. But I never fully connected to my Jewish roots for several reasons.

First, my parents were not religious and rarely went to temple. My father's greatest joy in being Jewish was to point out to me all the famous Jews that were in entertainment and sports. "Kirk Douglas, did you know that he was Jewish?" he would say with a smile on his face. "Did you know that Bernie Schwartz was Tony Curtis' real name?" was another one of his favorite refrains. Not to mention the bragging rights he claimed when it came to someone like Sandy Koufax, a Hall of Fame pitcher on the Dodgers who would not pitch on the Sabbath during the critical World Series.

My favorite pastime was to tease him about his hobby. "Hey Dad, what about John Wayne? Was he Jewish? Was his original name Hymie Goldberg?" I would ask with a lot of love in my heart. To this day, in memory of my old man, I carry on the Cohen tradition of pointing out to my friends and family all the famous Jews who are making the headlines and say to myself, "This one's for you, Dad!"

There were certain paradoxes that even the most religious members of my family displayed, which also made it difficult for me to relate to Judaism. For instance, my Aunt Muriel and Uncle Larry were strictly kosher, but I remember many Sundays when they would invite us out to their favorite Chinese restaurant. There, we ate delicious roast pork and spare ribs, strictly forbidden by kosher law. When I questioned them about this contradiction, they told me that it was all right for them to eat this food at the restaurant as long as they kept kosher at home. This never made any sense to me.

For all of these reasons, I never identified with my Jewish heritage. Years later, though, I would awaken to my spirituality. This awakening would radically change the course of my life.

* * * * *

When it was time to leave for college, I looked forward to the freedom and independence that awaited me. But as it turned out, I was caught in that awkward in-between place of vulnerable adolescence and was ill prepared to handle the emotional trauma that sometimes occurs when one leaves home for the first time. My roommate, although a nice guy, was more than a little untidy, leaving his dirty underwear and clothes strewn everywhere around the room. This went against my grain, my mother having run a pretty tight ship when I was growing up, assigning cleaning chores to my sister and me, and otherwise taking steps to make certain that the apartment always appeared immaculate. Needless to say, it didn't take much for me to move in with the girl whom I had just started dating.

This pattern of rushing into relationships, "fiercely and blindly," as one therapist put it, would continue to repeat itself in the years that followed. It would not be resolved until I finally made the effort to delve deeply into my psyche and heal the underlying emotional scars that were triggering my impulsive behavior.

The relationship with my girlfriend provided me with a sense of security and warmth, a safe haven from the stress of college life. Slowly, I cut off all ties to my family and friends because they didn't approve of my serious relationship that in their eyes had developed too quickly, particularly considering my age. But I shut my eyes and ears to them. I was content to center my life around this talented young music major, an aspiring concert pianist, who knew how to play on the heartstrings of my heart, not to mention my hormones. This isolation from my support group would come back to haunt me later as still another stress that would take me down the road of hopelessness and despair.

The academic demands and rigors of college life were additional stresses. Having entered college with excellent grades, I decided to become a veterinarian because I had always felt a connection with the animal kingdom whose unconditional love and devotion can be a great source of comfort. I have found that we cannot underestimate the many healing benefits that pets can offer us.

An article in a recent medical journal stated that those people with rheumatoid arthritis who owned pets had a significant decrease in joint pain involving their hands compared with people who did not own them. The authors of the study speculated that this may have been due to the increased activity of petting the animals, which then led to increased mobility and decreased stiffness in their hands. I think, though, that it was also the pure love and devotion that they received from their pets that triggered the beneficial physiological changes.

Another study revealed that dogs can detect the very early stages of cancer even earlier than the most sensitive diagnostic tests. They can also somehow sense when the blood sugar is dropping to dangerously low levels in diabetic patients, and, once trained to do so, immediately alert their owners who may be too confused themselves to realize this because of the effects that low blood sugar has on the brain. Even more fascinating is the fact that it has been shown in the past few years that people with psychiatric disorders like depression, anxiety, and even schizophrenia have marked improvement in their mental health thanks to man's best friend.

The use of "psychiatric service dogs" was conceived by Dr. Joan Esnayra, a forty-two-year-old geneticist with bipolar disorder who, in 2002, founded the Psychiatric Service Dog Society. These specially trained service dogs can alleviate mental health problems by helping patients remember to take their medication, stick to daily schedules, and navigate stressful situations in general. Just as dogs can sense when a diabetic's blood sugar is dropping, they also have an uncanny ability to sense their master's panic attacks before they happen, giving the individual the option to remove himself from the situation and/or take medication. From my own personal experience, I can attest that the dogs that I have owned throughout my life have been incredibly helpful in reducing my stress and anxiety.

At the beginning of my freshman year however, I had

a sobering experience that put a damper on my dream of becoming a veterinarian. Even though I had been in the top fifty of my graduating high school class of over a thousand students, I quickly came to realize that so were all of the other students sitting next to me in the huge, impersonal lecture halls where we learned about species and phylum in the premed biology classes. It was in these classes that I learned firsthand about Darwin's principle, *Survival of the Fittest*, and it was not through the lectures of my professor, but through the day-to-day experiences with my fellow classmates. The world of academia was an extremely competitive environment with students vying for the highest grades that would boost their chances for getting into the limited seats available at the various medical schools.

Though my relationship with my girlfriend was a source of calm and peace, it didn't take long for a storm to start brewing in my academic world. There was a tremendous amount of information to memorize in my biology and chemistry classes and this soon became quite overwhelming for me. I always had a low tolerance for stress and my parents took measures to ameliorate this problem in my younger years. I was a type A, high-maintenance, anxious child who always strived to succeed and constantly worried that I would be a failure.

I remember as if it were yesterday, coming home from school every Friday when I was in sixth grade and doing my homework while my friends were outside playing. I was obsessed by the fear that that if I did not do it immediately, I might be left to face it on Sunday night, a possibility that gave me panic attacks! Because of this, as I was growing up my life was lived according to a very rigid schedule, the days divided into pie charts with each activity allotted a precise slice of time. Being late was never an option for me.

Even as a young child, I used to go to sleep wearing my watch so that I would know the exact time when I got up in the morning. This habit came to an abrupt end when I awoke one morning and found my wristwatch wrapped around my ankle!

If I had a project that required certain supplies and equipment that were not readily at hand, my anxiety was often so great that my parents would rush out right away to get me all the supplies that I needed. Throughout my life, my mother was fond of reminding me that my fifth-grade teacher, Mrs. Preminger, once said that I was a "walking time bomb." My inability to effectively cope with stress manifested physically with repeated episodes of asthma attacks that required many urgent visits to my pediatrician.

Although my parents were well meaning in their attempts to shield me from stress, I reached young adulthood unprepared to handle the stresses and challenges that awaited me. Ultimately, the academic load in these premed science classes became so burdensome that I finally made the monumental decision of surrendering my dream of becoming a veterinarian and following another one of my passions: languages. I majored in Spanish and minored in French with the intention of teaching English as a second language to Spanish-speaking people. As I made the transition to the world of language and linguistics, I breathed a sigh of relief and felt a sense of freedom. Ironically, although I never became a language teacher, my knowledge of Spanish would serve me very well later in my career.

However, even though I was enjoying my new classes, in my third year of college, I began to slowly sink into the quicksand of depression. My decision to live off campus with my girlfriend that year added to a sense of isolation that was intensified when my love for her began to crumble. For two years I had built my world around this woman, cutting off both my family and friends who did not approve of this relationship. Whether this waning of my love for her was a triggering factor for my depression or a symptom of my depression I am not sure, but it certainly accelerated my descent into madness.

On a subconscious level, I was also carrying a measure of guilt in my heart for having changed my major from premed to Spanish. Even though my parents never actually said that they wanted me to go into the medical field, there was nonetheless an unspoken expectation that this was the course my life should take. The thought that I had disappointed them, especially my mother, weighed heavily on my heart.

The first stirrings of this downward spiral into the world of hopelessness and despair started with my inability to sleep, a common symptom of depression. Days of little or no sleep led me into a world known to psychiatrists as "anhedonia," where there was no joy, no happiness – a hollow hell of emptiness, darkness, and gloom. On one occasion, I attempted to jump-start myself out of this state of emotional numbness by eating some ice cream. Try as I might, the experience elicited no pleasure, no taste of sweetness. As autumn turned to winter, I felt increasingly dead inside. Finally, I decided to go see a guidance counselor. We had a few sessions, but I could not get in touch with my feelings or the reasons for my deep sadness. The therapist was sincere and dedicated, but he didn't understand the magnitude and depth of my quandary. Neither did I.

As I became more and more desperate, I began to act out my suicidal impulses. I toyed with a razor blade and cut my wrists, but the wounds were only superficial. They did no real physical harm, but the damage to my soul was deep. I then tied a plastic bag around my head and tried to knock myself unconscious in hopes that I would suffocate. Finally, in my last act of desperation, I climbed to the nineteenth floor of the dormitory tower, squeezed myself through the window, and prepared to jump. Somehow, my therapist was alerted to my situation and came running to my rescue. He called to me with a mix of desperation and relief in his voice as I grabbed his hand and took my first steps towards my recovery.

* * * * *

I was taken to the school infirmary where a doctor immediately called my parents to tell them what had happened. My mom and dad jumped into the car and broke all land speed records on their 150-mile journey from New York City to Albany. I saw fear and apprehension in their eyes when they first came into my room. Having no idea of the destructive path that I had been following, they were not emotionally prepared to handle the situation, especially my mother.

Throughout my life, whenever I tried to express any negative feelings such as sadness or discouragement, Mom would quickly change the topic of our conversation. As a result, having learned to suppress my feelings, I lived in a world of denial in which I was literally unable to confront my inner demons.

Having a demanding and emotionally distant mother left deep scars on my psyche, which was a central factor that would lead to my lifelong struggle with depression. While in junior high school, I told her that I had received a grade of 98 on a geometry test, to which she replied, "What, you couldn't get 100?" Comments like this meant that I spent most of my life trying to please someone who made it impossible because of her own emotional scars. When, eventually, I made peace with her, I reached a major turning point in my healing.

As we made the trip back to my home to Queens, I did not know what the next step would be. I was too numb to care. My parents took me to a psychiatric hospital located on Long Island where a woman interviewed me and took us on a tour of the well-tended hospital grounds. Bored and restless by a visit that seemed pointless to me, I was prepared to leave when I discovered that that was not an option. The next thing I knew, she was leading me to the locked unit of the psychiatric ward for patients who were a danger to themselves or others. I was chilled to the bone when the door slammed shut behind me and I realized that I had lost my freedom. My parents quietly sobbed as I disappeared from their view.

Since I was non-communicative, too tired, and too drained to effectively discuss my problems and feelings, and also because I was at the age when a psychotic break typically first occurs, I was diagnosed as being schizophrenic and was promptly started on a powerful antipsychotic medication, Thorazine®. It didn't take long for the medication to turn me into a zombie as I wandered around the ward in a haze for days. I also became incontinent thanks to this medication. I remember one night tearing off my soiled bed sheets and stumbling down the hallway to toss them into the communal washer on the ward. It was a living nightmare.

Fortunately, the psychiatrist finally noted that I was not responding to treatment and reevaluated my case. My diagnosis was changed to major depression and he started me on one of the tricyclic antidepressants that were in vogue at that time.

Later in my medical training, I would learn that tricyclic antidepressants were highly effective in the treatment of depression. Unfortunately, they had some bothersome side effects, many of which I experienced, such as dry mouth, blurry vision, difficulty urinating, rapid heart rate, and constipation, just to name a few. It was because of these side effects and not because of the poor therapeutic response to these drugs that a whole new generation of antidepressant medications, known as selective serotonin reuptake inhibitors, or SSRIs, was spawned. This class of medications includes drugs such as Paxil®, Prozac®, and Zoloft®, which are free of the problems associated with the tricyclics, although they do have their own profile of side effects.

As the haze from the Thorazine® faded, and the therapeutic effects of the tricyclic antidepressant started to kick in, my mood and alertness began to improve. But the improvement was temporary; more episodes of suicidal depression awaited me in the years that followed. However for now, I savored the return of my sanity.

An unexpected benefit of my improved mental state was that I became aware of the Ping-Pong table on the unit.

Since there was downtime at night and not much else to do, I started to play the game of table tennis and became quite proficient at this sport. Ironically enough, this was a skill that would accompany me throughout the following important years of my life when I became the number one seeded table tennis champ both in medical school and, after that, my family practice residency program. Whenever my fellow classmates and doctors-to-be inquired as to how I became so adept at this game, I would just smile, never letting them in on the truth of the humble roots of my Ping-Pong greatness.

My fellow patients on the floor were a fascinating conglomeration of people. One who clearly stands out in my memory and still brings a smile to my face was an adolescent Hassidic, Abraham. He was clothed in full Hassidic garb, wearing a skullcap called a *yahmaca*, with a *talus,* or prayer shawl, draped over his shoulders, his long wispy sideburns wrapped around his ears, prayer book in his hand, constantly *dovening*, the Jewish tradition of repeated bowing while praying, saying the words, "don't touch" over and over again as he then proceeded to continually touch people, especially women.

I was never quite sure why young Abraham was on a locked unit because he did not appear to be a danger to himself or anybody else. Certainly, he was an interesting character, one who definitely added a distinctive flavor to the brew of patients stewing on the unit. Although Abraham was a little tiresome with his nonstop mantra, there was something very endearing about him and I soon found myself empathizing with his difficult situation.

There was another patient whose oft-repeated words stand out in my mind: "Once you get into one of these places, it is like a revolving door; you just keep coming back, again and again." Although I refused to believe him, being quite frightened at that prospect, his ominous words pointed to what the future had in store for me.

I found the treatment programs on the psychiatric unit to be well run and organized. There was daily group therapy as well as sessions with the psychiatrist who had been assigned to us to monitor our response to the medications. As my mental clarity continued to improve, I became more active in my healthcare and recovery. I was also granted more freedom and liberties. This included being allowed to leave the locked unit and walk around the hospital grounds, first with an attendant and then by myself.

I was also able to eat at the hospital cafeteria where, contrary to popular belief, the food was quite good, particularly when compared with the bland food served on the unit. The was important to me at the time because my improved mood was also accompanied by a greatly improved appetite. As my optimism, joy, good humor, and zest for life finally returned to me, the endless nightmare of dark despair that had held me prisoner for so long came to an end.

The final test of my ability to cope with independence involved an unsupervised trip to New York City for dinner and sightseeing together with a group of other patients who were about to be discharged. This gift of freedom filled me with intoxicating joy. Even the simple act of taking a subway was an exhilarating event. The trip was a complete success as we returned triumphantly to the hospital. After my two-week stay, I was ready for discharge and the next chapter of my life was waiting to be written.

Chapter Two

Following my discharge from the hospital in early January 1974, I was brimming with intense excitement as I jumped back into the rhythm of life, happy to be back home with my parents and living in my small but comfortable bedroom that was filled with so many wonderful childhood memories. I decided to attend a local school, Queens College. This was a city university that offered free tuition to residents of NYC – a bargain that I couldn't turn down. Since it was too late to register, I decided to audit several Spanish classes. One was an advanced grammar course, which I ended up acing.

When the course ended, the professor advised me to register for his class the following semester, saying that he would give me the A that I had earned without my having to attend the class again. This was an offer that I happily accepted. I also audited a Spanish literature class where, destiny intervening, I met my first wife.

At Queens College, a layer of shyness was peeled away and I became an outgoing, confident young man. As a volunteer at the YMCA, I was an assistant to a gym teacher in a children's fitness program, a job that I loved. And as a cub reporter for the school newspaper, I also ventured into the world of journalism. In between these pursuits, I donned a white hat and apron and worked in the school cafeteria serving up burgers and fries to my hungry classmates.

When I matriculated the following semester, I made a decision that would be a turning point in my life; I set my sights on becoming a medical doctor. The fact that science, especially biology, had always fascinated me was one driving force behind my decision. More importantly, I wanted to help people. I still loved animals but believe it or not, it was easier for me at the time to get accepted to medical school than to veterinary school. Because of my love for languages, I decided to keep Spanish as my major while also taking all of the required premed courses.

There was a lot of catching up to do. While at Albany, I enrolled in only a handful of these courses. Now, in order to gain admission to medical school, I had to condense two years of the premedical curriculum into one year. I entered into this endeavor with joy and sense of purpose.

Immersing myself in Spanish and then diving into my biology and chemistry classes, subjects that required a completely different mind-set, was challenging but fun. I did extremely well in all of my premedical courses, including the make or break class organic chemistry, in which a grade of B or better was required in order to have a chance at acceptance to medical school. When I learned that I had received a grade of B+, I breathed a deep sigh of relief.

Another part of the requirement for entrance into medical school was the Medical College Admission Test, usually referred to as MCAT, which covered four subjects in a multiple-choice format: math, science, English, and general knowledge. During the summer prior to applying for admission to medical school, I took an intensive MCAT review course, studying eight hours a day, five days a week. All of this hard work paid off when I received high scores on this important exam.

Applying to over thirty medical schools, I was thrilled when, early in my senior year, I received a request for an interview at the Medical College of Wisconsin, located in Milwaukee. My dad, a sharp dresser himself, bought me my dark brown corduroy "interview suit." He beamed with pride when I set off on my maiden flight to Milwaukee. "No more virgin on the ground, and now, no more virgin in the air," he joked. It was a happy time for both of us. The interview went very well and after returning home, I began to check the mail on a daily basis, praying that

I would find an acceptance notice.

A few weeks later a letter arrived. At the time, I was staying with my Aunt Mary who lived within walking distance of Queens College. One night when I returned late from a chemistry lab, she was waiting for me, phone in hand. It seemed that this letter was from that medical school, and I had been accepted. My dear friend Ricky, whom I had known since we both had been in diapers, took the phone to describe the joyful scene of my parents hugging one another as tears ran down their cheeks.

After that acceptance I knew that my life would be changed forever, although little did I know how much. At the time, I was only aware of an incredible sense of accomplishment mixed with gratitude that I had been given this opportunity. Even though I was accepted by other schools, SUNY, the State University of New York at Stony Brook School of Medicine would be my ultimate destination. I was attracted to this school because of its unique and innovative philosophy about the practice of medicine. I also liked the fact that it was a small class. Although the average medical school class consisted of one hundred students or more, the fifty students I would eventually join were evenly divided between men and women.

In addition to my MCAT scores and grade point average, I caught the school's attention for two other reasons. First, I was a Spanish major, and that was unique. Then, when asked by the professor who was interviewing me to tell him something interesting about myself, I cautiously informed him that I was into transcendental meditation, at which he sat back in his chair, stroked his beard, and, smiling, asked me to tell him something else interesting about myself. A week later, I received my acceptance notice.

With my future secured, I proposed to the girl I had been dating for the past two years. She accepted and we planned on marrying after the first year of medical school. Our families rejoiced at the news. So, off I went to Stony Brook, confident that I was ready for anything. Or at least that's what I thought.

* * * * *

I was excited and had great expectations as I started my first year of medical school in early September 1976. I always enjoyed the north end of Long Island where Stony Brook was situated. During my first year, I roomed with three of my classmates in a beautiful house located on a cliff overlooking Long Island Sound. I found it incredibly soothing to be so close to the water. The fresh salt air was refreshing and invigorating after a day spent in a stuffy classroom or a formaldehyde-filled gross anatomy lab.

I got along well with all of my housemates. In particular, I became good friends with Gary who lived in the loft on the second floor. He was one of those geniuses who absorbed all the material when it was presented in class and never needed to study. Every night before an exam while we were all studying feverishly, Gary would be upstairs practicing his putting. His easygoing, warm manner always put me at ease.

Gary's love of sports also had a positive influence. Not only did he re-ignite my passion for golf, providing me with a release from all the stress and strain of medical school, but with his encouragement, I also started to jog on a regular basis. I remember one unforgettable morning when it was finally time to make the seven-mile run from home to medical school. Before leaving, we blasted the theme song from the movie *Rocky,* not caring that we woke our roommates from a sound sleep. We needed the inspiration to begin this monumental journey. After we were fully pumped up, Gary and I completed the epic run and made it into the annals of jogging history. That was thirty years ago and the thrill of this accomplishment still stands out in my mind.

My class was composed of an eclectic mix of people from all different walks of life, but since we spent eight hours a day, five days a week, huddled together in lecture halls, we became like family. Medical school was even more of a full-time job than I imagined it would be. There was an enormous amount of material to digest and I hungrily devoured this vast amount of knowledge that I found to be fascinating and challenging.

It was during medical school when I started to study the anatomy of the human body, so intricately and perfectly designed, that I had to believe that a Higher Source had created this fascinating, complex wonder of nature. One only needed to look at the anatomy of a single cell, which is like a universe unto itself, to fully appreciate the amazing creation that we call Life. On a microscopic level, each cell contains a vast array of structures that have precise functions and exotic names such as the endoplasmic reticulum, Golgi bodies, mitochondria, cytoskeleton, ribosomes, centrosomes, lysosomes, and peroxisomes. I found the graceful dance and interplay between of all the structures of the human body truly extraordinary and inspiring.

Although I enjoyed all of the fascinating material that was being presented to me, the study of gross anatomy induced a mini-crisis. Confronted with such a massive amount of information, I became too anxious to study, convinced that I could never memorize the names and functions of the 650 muscles, 206 bones and hundreds of nerves that make up the human body. Out of desperation, I went to see the professor and told him that I was going to fail his class because my memory banks were short-circuiting from data overload. He must have heard this plea many times before because he just chuckled, waved his hand and said, "Don't worry, you'll do fine." And fortunately, he was right. I did extremely well on the exam.

For a while, my confidence was boosted until my third year of medical school when, overwhelmed by anxiety, I would drive my car at full speed headlong into a stone overpass in a desperate attempt to put an end to my life.

That year began peacefully enough for me. It was now time to leave the classroom and continue my education in the various hospitals affiliated with the medical school, rotating through all of the various subspecialties in order to apply all that we had learned during our first two years of school. I eagerly looked forward to this opportunity.

Meanwhile, everything was also going well at home. My wife and I had been married for one year and were enjoying our life together. But a dark cloud was looming on the horizon. Soon, this tranquil time would be obliterated when I began my first rotation in the fall of 1978. Although these rotations were just an introduction to the different fields of medicine, any of which it would take years of experience to become skilled in, I put the undue burden upon myself of trying to master every specialty in the short time that I was at the various hospitals.

In hindsight, this was an unrealistic expectation. However, at the time, I enthusiastically embraced the challenge until gradually I realized that I would never accomplish this goal. It was then that anxiety began to incapacitate me. Slowly, my sanity began to unravel, one thread at a time.

Sleep became impossible. Each night when I returned home from the hospital, I would put on my sweats and jog for miles, hoping that when bedtime arrived, I would collapse from exhaustion. But the fear of failure kept me frozen in a state of wakefulness night after night until finally I made my plan to escape this relentless torture once and for all.

One winter morning, I wrote a suicide note, got into my car, the weapon that I had decided to use to end my life, and drove in the direction of the hospital. Entering the parkway, I accelerated to maximum speed and set my sights on the stone overpass that lay ahead. Two hundred yards. One hundred. Fifty. The next thing I remember was waking up in the intensive care unit of the hospital with doctors and family members hovering anxiously over my bedside.

Initially, nobody knew that I had deliberately tried to take my life until my wife found the suicide note at home. She was beside herself. I had not wanted to burden her with my grief, so I concealed my innermost thoughts. My wife had no idea of the depth of my despair. My car was crushed by the impact and it was miraculous that I had only sustained relatively minor injuries. These included a concussion, the amputation of the distal aspect of my right index finger, fractures of my right clavicle and right foot, and a flattened nose that would require plastic surgery.

After my condition stabilized, I was transferred to the psychiatric ward and languished there for over a week. I had given up all hope and was filled with gloom and hopelessness. The antidepressant prescribed for me provided no relief. As my mental state continued to seriously deteriorate, the psychiatrist suggested that I have a course of electroconvulsive therapy in an attempt to pull me out of the deep depression that was swallowing me up. I was willing to do anything that would free me from the nightmare in which I was trapped.

ECT invokes fearful images for some people; however it can be a relatively safe and effective therapy for the treatment of severe depression. During ECT treatment, a short-acting barbiturate is used to induce unconsciousness, in conjunction with succinlycholine, a muscle relaxer, to minimize any muscle trauma from the procedure. A seizure is then induced that could be as minor as the slight twitch of the big toe. Although no one knows the exact mechanism by which ECT works, it is theorized that a series of these minor seizures alter the brain chemistry in such a way that it leads to a significant improvement in a patient's mood. The most common side effect is short-term memory loss. There can be more serious side effects, although these are relatively uncommon.

The history of the use of ECT in the treatment of severe depression is remarkable. In the past, it was noted that people with epilepsy or seizure disorders had a lower incidence of clinical depression than the general population. It was then reasoned that by inducing a seizure, major depression could be ameliorated. Empiric observation proved to be correct and over the years, as the techniques used in

ECT have become more refined, this therapy has helped thousands of people who have suffered from life-threatening depression. This certainly was true in my case.

With each treatment, I returned miraculously from the land of the dead. I began to look forward to my ECT sessions. I once amused my psychiatrist by telling him, just before the procedure was about to begin, to give it "all you got!" Fortunately, after completing a series of treatments, my condition markedly improved. The furthest thing from my mind at the time was that this was only the beginning of the thirty ECT treatments that awaited me in the years ahead. I was discharged after a two-week stay and couldn't wait to get back to medical school.

* * * * *

I returned to medical school in January 1979 overflowing with tremendous joy, and was able to make up the time that I lost while I was away. Rotating through the various subspecialties in the many hospitals that were scattered throughout Long Island was a great learning experience that I relished.

An incident that I will never forget occurred one day in a hospital where I was studying nephrology. During a break, having decided to explore the other medical floors, I wandered onto the maternity ward. There, I observed for the first time an amazing event, the birth of a child. I was so elated that I could not stop smiling from ear to ear. When I rejoined my colleagues, our instructor, clearly accustomed to the delight that students experienced on these occasions said to me, "Looks like you just witnessed your first birth."

During my fourth year of medical school, spring 1980, it was time for me to start interviewing for my residency programs. Initially, I wanted to be a pediatrician because I enjoyed working with children. However, it was during the first few months of a summer internship with a family practitioner that I changed my mind. Intrigued by the relationship between family dynamics and its effect on the health and well-being of all members of the family, I decided to switch my specialty from pediatrics to family medicine. This specialty would also increase the scope of my practice by allowing me to address the health concerns of both men and women. As importantly, I could also take care of children in my practice. I applied to several programs in the northeast and anxiously awaited their reply.

My first interview was in Massachusetts where I stayed with a family practice resident from the program who graciously welcomed me into his home. This visit opened up a new door for me, and once I passed through this portal, my life would be changed forever.

During my stay I was fascinated by the fact that, despite a busy on-call schedule, my host still found the time to meditate at least two hours both in the morning and evening. When I questioned him about this, he told me about his guru in India who had taught him how to see the "Inner Light" and hear the "Inner Sound" through meditation.

Up until that time, I little interest in anything related to spirituality. Now, after hearing his words, it was as though a light flashed on illuminating some long ago forgotten memory that was hidden in the recesses of my mind. The concept of the Inner Light and Inner Sound rang true within the core of my being, a core that up until that point, I had been completely unaware of.

On returning home, I immediately contacted my friend Larry, a fellow medical student, who was also at the beginning of his spiritual awakening and shared all that I had learned with him. Thinking about the wonders of the spiritual realm filled me with indescribable joy and peace. In my excitement, I said that we had to pack our bags right away and travel to India in order to study with this guru.

He was very interested in what I had to say and called several days later to tell me about a program that would teach us how to contact our own inner guru. These teachings were to be found in a book entitled *A Course in Miracles,* written by a psychologist who said that Jesus had guided her during the writing of this book. I was fascinated and wanted to know as much as possible about the Course.

Consequently, Larry and I attended a seminar based on these teachings. I became disillusioned when I noticed that the instructor leading this group was smoking, a practice that ran contrary to my beliefs because in my mind, it was essential to keep the body as pure as possible in order to nurture spiritual growth. When asked about this apparent contradiction, the instructor explained that it was not he who was smoking but rather his body.

His rationalization turned me off to these teachings. In retrospect, however, I realized that by judging this man I turned away from the valuable information contained in the *Course in Miracles.* This was a lesson that I would not soon forget.

While continuing his exploration of the spiritual realms, Larry came across a book published by the Summit University Press called *The Chela and the Path* by the ascended master El Morya. I never had heard of the term "ascended master," but his words struck my heart like a bolt of lightning that electrified my soul. This book would lead me on an amazing spiritual journey that would span the next fifteen years of my life. The awakening to my spiritual path would also lead to the end of my marriage.

After graduating from medical school in the spring of 1980, Larry left for the West Coast. I began my residency at Southside Hospital in Bay Shore, New York and this program took precedence in my life. As a result, my spiritual quest was temporarily put on the back burner. I was excited to actually start "playing doctor" and finally put into action what I had been studying for the last four years.

I thrived on the frenetic, hectic pace of life that was part and parcel of being a first-year resident, during which time I was on call every third night. This meant that often I would work almost nonstop for thirty hours with little to no sleep. After the shift was over, I would go home, grunt hello to my wife, and then collapse into bed, sleeping for the next twelve hours. I loved it! These three years at the hospital, though exciting, went by so fast that in retrospect, most of it seems like a blur to me now.

I also worked in a local health center where I had an outpatient practice. This facility was located in the largest Hispanic community on Long Island and it was here that I put my knowledge of Spanish to good use. Many of the patients were indigent and could not speak English. When I spoke to them in their native tongue, all language barriers disappeared and a bond of trust and goodwill was forged between us.

There were many aspects of this part of my residency program that I enjoyed. What I loved most, though, was taking care of the newborns at the center and watching them develop into feisty toddlers, each with their own distinct personality. As they got older, I tried to involve them in their examination by putting my stethoscope in their ears and watching their faces light up when they heard their own heartbeat for the first time. I loved to tease them, telling them silly jokes to make them laugh and taking great delight in hearing them giggle

I made a special effort to treat these little ones with respect, not talking down to them. From my experience, I had found that children are highly impressionable, especially up to the age of seven, absorbing everything parents and adults say to them. These remarks shape their perceptions of who they are and how they perceive the world around them. If they are treated harshly, the damage to their psyche and self-esteem can be deep and long lasting.

As part of our three-year training as family practice residents, we had to deliver thirty babies. The most important thing that I learned from this experience was that I did not deliver the baby; it was the mother who did all the hard work to give birth to her child. I was there just to catch the infant and make sure that it didn't fall on the floor on the way out. Still, it was a thrill for me to be part of this momentous occasion.

The one part that I did not enjoy, however, was having to circumcise the male newborns whom I had helped deliver the night before. After a night of little sleep, it was particularly difficult for me to subject this precious infant, barely hours old, to what I considered to be a horrific procedure. Back in those days, it was thought by those in the know in the medical community, that newborns could not feel pain because their brains were not fully developed. Therefore, not only circumcisions, but even open-heart surgery was done without anesthesia. Now, thankfully, an injection can be given that numbs the nerve which supplies the foreskin. However, twenty-five years ago, that was not the case.

I cringed each time I had to perform this procedure, praying that when it was over I had not changed the sex of the poor baby. Fortunately, that never happened. The one thing that I learned from this whole experience was that I was never cut out to be a *Moyle*.

There was, however, one frightening moment that occurred while I was covering the obstetrics unit, which almost caused me to walk away from the medical profession and hang up my stethoscope for good. This harrowing event began one night when I was called by the nurses on the maternity ward to examine a young girl who early in the last trimester of her pregnancy had gone into labor, having been prevented by her drug addiction from seeking prenatal care. When I did a pelvic exam to see how close she was to delivery, I felt a large balloon-like thin membrane of a sort that I had never encountered previously. Realizing that further investigation was needed, I inserted a metal speculum, only to hear a popping sound, followed by a gush of amniotic fluid. The umbilical cord then prolapsed, endangering the precious flow of oxygen to the baby. Because of my inexperience, I had triggered a medical emergency!

A team of attending physicians came rushing in to the hospital and took her immediately into the OR for an emergency Caesarean section. The child was born prematurely, which increased the risk for neurological damage and other serious complications. Crushed, I felt as though I no longer deserved to be a doctor.

Seeing me in this state of despair, one of the attending physicians put his arm around me and said that what I palpated during my exam of this patient were called hourglass membranes and they were going to pop any minute no matter what I had done. His words helped lighten the guilt and sorrow that were weighing heavily on my heart. I was also comforted when I learned, later on in my residency program, that the child was developing normally with no evidence of neurological impairment.

At the beginning of the second year of the residency program, it was my turn to be on the other end of the table when my wife was about to give birth to our baby. Even though by this time I had been involved in many deliveries, it was difficult to be calm and objective when it came to the birth of my own child. In reality, I was extremely nervous because I knew of all the potential complications that could occur during childbirth. When the first twinges of labor began, I rushed my wife to the hospital. Our obstetrician, a kind and understanding man, told me after examining her, to take my wife home, adding that she still had a long way to go.

Hours later, my wife's labor did progress and this time when we went to the hospital, we were not turned away. Standing by her side, rubbing her back, and murmuring words of encouragement, I anxiously waited for the momentous moment of the birth of our child. Finally, just after midnight on July 10, 1981, my sweet baby girl, Staci Renee Cohen, made her entrance into the world. I could not stop smiling as tears of joy came to my eyes when I held her in my arms for the first time.

As soon as I could, I called my parents, who lived about an hour away, to give them the good news. Since it was late at night, I told them to wait until morning to see their first grandchild. However, in their excitement and without telling me of their intentions, they rushed to the hospital. My heart melted when I saw them standing outside the door of the delivery room, smiles glued to their faces, as their new granddaughter was rolled out.

On the way home from the hospital, I turned on the radio and joined Stevie Wonder in the song that he wrote celebrating the birth of his daughter: "Isn't She Lovely?" Turning up the volume, I sung it with full gusto, slightly out of key, but since the windows were rolled up, I just continued to belt it out. I couldn't be happier.

Chapter Three

In the second year of my residency program, my call schedule was reduced to every fourth night and, as family life was settling down, I had more time to pursue my spiritual studies. As a result, I ordered more books from the Summit University Press, some of which contained the teachings of Jesus. This was disconcerting for my wife because she had been raised in a traditional Jewish household where anything related to Christianity was banned. Through the years, it seemed to me that many Jews for some reason, feel threatened even by the mere mention of Jesus' name. I felt the same way until I had my spiritual awakening.

From all that I had read, it was apparent to me that Jesus was one the greatest Rabbis who had ever lived. But although I explained this to my wife, nothing could assuage her concerns. The anger and scorn that she heaped upon me because of my desire to cross the boundaries of Judaism became a heavy cross of guilt that I carried for many years. And the deeper I ventured into the uncharted realms of spiritual teachings, the deeper the rift became between us.

The Summit University Press was the publishing arm of a church that was centered in Malibu, California. This organization offered monthly lessons that included such topics as karma, reincarnation, chakras, the science of the spoken word, and the power of prayer. There were also fascinating information on the mystical teachings of Christianity, Judaism, Hinduism and Buddhism, including the Gnostic Gospels, the Kabbalah, the sacred Hindu text *The Bhagavad-Gita,* and the Eightfold Path of Gautama Buddha.

These monthly lessons from the church only whetted my appetite for more information, naïvely thinking that when I reached a critical mass of knowledge, it would automatically qualify me for entrance into the blissful realms of nirvana. However, in the years that followed, Life would teach me that knowledge alone did not equate to spiritual enlightenment. I would first have to clean up the emotional debris that cluttered my psyche before I could truly assimilate the wisdom, peace, and joy that these spiritual teachings were offering me.

Still, in my enthusiasm to take the express train to heaven, I did everything I could to accelerate my spiritual growth. And since this included becoming a vegetarian, I learned how to cook great veggie chili and became adept in the preparation of a variety of dishes featuring tofu and tempeh. At the hospital where I spent most of my time during my residency program, the cafeteria did not offer many choices for my new diet, so I became a "junk food" vegetarian, consuming endless greasy grilled cheese sandwiches and massive quantities of French fries.

Although I had hoped that my wife would share in my excitement and that we could walk this path together, I discovered that it only infuriated her, as did my change in diet. She seemed threatened and was angered by my attempt to break away from the confines of Judaism to explore other realms of spiritual beliefs. My wife was also jealous of the joy that the monthly lessons brought me.

I started to apply the principles that I was learning, especially the power of prayer. During the second year of my residency program, I was taking care of an elderly woman who was diagnosed with an advanced case of multiple myeloma, a malignancy of certain blood cells called plasma cells. Her rib cage was riddled with multiple pathological fractures and punched out bony lesions. This woman's prognosis, even with aggressive treatment, was dismal. After I referred her to the oncologist, she was "lost to follow-up" as we say in medical jargon and I did not see her again for over a year. But I continued to pray for her.

One day, I looked across the waiting room in the clinic and saw her seated there. When we hugged one another, she wept as she told me that she had made a complete recovery from this devastating disease. In my heart, I believed that prayer played some part in her remarkable healing. This had to be one of the most poignant moments of my residency program. Years later, the power of prayer would save my own life.

Later on in my career, I was pleased to find out about a fascinating study done by the cardiologist Robert Byrd in 1988, which scientifically demonstrated the healing power of prayer. This study, which involved 393 patients at San Francisco's General Hospital Coronary Care Unit, looked at the effect of prayer carried out by a distance by several home prayer groups. The 393 subjects were divided into a group of 192 patients who were prayed for by four to seven different people and a control group of 201 people who did not have any benefit of prayer. It was a double-blind placebo study, considered the "gold standard" in clinical trials. This meant that neither the physician nor the patients knew who belonged to which group. The results were astounding. The prayed-for patients were five times less likely to require antibiotics and three times less likely to develop pulmonary edema, both statistically significant results.

I also learned that the healing effects of prayer could be explained scientifically through quantum physics. This is a fascinating field of science that explores the makeup of the subatomic world. The quantum world exists in a dimension not mediated by time or space. This dimension is referred to as nonlocal. Prayer works at this nonlocal level, which is why when someone prays for you at a distance, with the purity of intent that is so vital to the effectiveness of prayer, it can have such potent, tangible effects.

I found it fascinating that as one delves deeper into the world of quantum physics, it becomes apparent that there is a Cosmic Intelligence, underlying and interconnecting all of Life on this planet and the Universe. Even the noted physicist Max Planck, a pioneer in the field of quantum physics, made reference to this fact in his acceptance speech for the Nobel Prize in the study of the atom when he said:

> *As a man who has devoted his whole life to the most clear headed science, to the study of matter, I can tell you as a result of my research about the atoms this much: "There is no matter as such!" All matter originates and exists only by virtue of a force which brings the particles of the atom to vibration and holds this most minute solar system of the atom together. We must assume behind this force the existence of a conscious and intelligent mind. This mind is the matrix of all matter.*
>
> (John Davidson,
> *The Secret of the Creative Vacuum*,
> The C.W. Daniel Company Limited, 1989)

* * * * *

The walls around my narrow view of the world continued to crumble as I was exposed to, what were for me, exciting new concepts. Now, another door was opening in my life that would lead me out of the constricted confines of conventional medicine into a whole new paradigm of healing since my spiritual awakening also stirred my interest in the field of alternative medicine.

An experience that I had with a patient in the third year of my residency reinforced my desire to learn other modalities in healing. A burly, strong, middle-aged butcher, he used to carry heavy sides of beef on his shoulders in and out of the freezer all day long. He had just had a myocardial infarction, more commonly known as a heart attack, when I first met him. Because of repeated episodes of chest pain, he had been advised by the cardiologists to undergo cardiac bypass surgery. I had built a rapport of trust with him so he turned to me for advice. Based on the training that I had at the time, I advised him to go through with the surgery. After this bypass, he became a changed man, merely a shadowy shell of his former self. My heart was filled with remorse when he mournfully said to me, "Doc, I don't know what they did to me, but I feel hollow inside."

When he said that, I felt that not only had I let him down, but that I had violated the Hippocratic oath, "First, do no harm," as well. I also noticed that some of my other patients were having side effects from the medications and treatments that were worse than the disease itself, observations that were verified recently when a study found that 100,000 people per year die as the result of side effects from prescription and over-the-counter medications. In addition, more than two million people a year are seriously harmed from these side effects. These figures become even more startling by the fact that people were not misusing or abusing these medications. The harm came from taking the drugs as directed. I am not against the use of medication for the treatment of disease. I feel, however, that it must be used judiciously and with respect.

As a physician, I wanted to follow the principles reflected in the words of Thomas Edison when he said, "The doctor of the future will give no medication but will instead educate the patient about the care of the human frame, in diet, and in the cause and prevention of disease."

I prayed to God to lead me to treatments that were safe, effective, and free of harmful side effects in which the cause of the disease and not just the symptoms would be addressed. My prayers were answered when the church introduced me to a vast array of alternative healing modalities including homeopathy, acupuncture, ayurvedic and nutritional medicine, macrobiotics, chelation therapy, natural or bio-identical hormones, iridology, foot reflexology, aromatherapy, Bach flower remedies, and the healing power of sound, music, and color, just to name a few. I eventually incorporated all of these healing modalities into my medical practice.

My introduction to these healing arts came about in the early 1980s when the stirrings of alternative medicine were just beginning. I was excited to join the pioneers in a field that had grown and flourished through a grass roots movement. A study done in 1990 by the *Journal of the American Medical Association*, a prestigious journal in the field of conventional medicine, revealed that more people were going to alternative healthcare providers than to their physicians and were spending billions of dollars out of pocket for these services. This confirmed what I already knew, but it certainly was a wake-up call for the medical profession.

I had a particular interest in homeopathy and later actually became certified in that field. Homeopathy recognizes that most disease (*dis*-ease), starts on the mental/emotional plane before eventually filtering into the physical plane to produce the symptoms of various illnesses. Since homeopathic remedies act on all three planes simultaneously, they can be highly effective in the treatment of depression when used under the guidance of an experienced homeopath. For this reason, I want to give more background information on this vital topic. I would also like to clear up some confusion concerning homeopathy.

In my experience, I had found that many people equated the term homeopathy with alternative medicine, which is incorrect. Many times, while I was in practice, patients had told me that they were looking for a "homeopathic" doctor, meaning that they actually wanted to be treated by a physician who practiced alternative medicine. Homeopathy is a distinct healing modality, one of the many healing arts that fall under the umbrella of alternative medicine.

Homeopathy dates back to the late eighteenth century when it was discovered and developed by Samuel Hanhemann, a physician who studied medicine at the Universities of Leipzig, Vienna and Erlanger. Although highly respected in professional circles for his papers on both medicine and chemistry, Hahnemann found the various medical therapies of his day, including bloodletting, cathartics, leeches, and the use of toxic chemicals, to be questionable treatments.

He left the practice of medicine to translate medical works and it was while reading Cullen's edition of the *Materia Medica* that Hahnemann came across records that discussed the use of Peruvian bark in the treatment of malaria. Cullen suggested that the healing properties of this substance derived from its bitterness. Hahnemann, not satisfied with this explanation and driven by his insatiable thirst for knowledge, ingested a sample of this bark in its raw state, whereupon he developed all of the symptoms of malaria. This led him to deduce that if a substance can cause symptoms in a healthy person, then this same substance could cure them in someone who was ill and displaying similar symptoms. Thus, the principle of "like cures like," also known as the Law of Similars, was born. The very definition of the word homeopathy reflects this principle: *homeo* – same, *pathy* – disease, or same as the disease.

As a scientist, Hahnemann and other like-minded physicians began systemically testing substances upon themselves and recording their observation in minute detail, including every mental, emotional, and physical symptom. This continued for a period of six years, during which time Hahnemann also compiled an exhaustive list of homeopathic remedies recorded by different doctors in different countries throughout the world that subsequently became the standard text for homeopathy. Applying the Law of Similars, he and his colleagues immediately began to see results that far surpassed those of his peers who were using the treatments previously described.

Interestingly enough, he noted that serial dilution and succussion, or shaking, of the remedies increased their therapeutic power and effectiveness. In fact, the most potent remedies were those in which the serial dilutions continued to the point where not even a single molecule of the original substance remained. What was contained in the remedy was the energy blueprint of the original substance and so homeopathy is a form of energy or vibrational medicine.

Hahnemann also recognized that the body has its own inherent healing power, known as the vital force that in traditional Chinese medicine is called Chi. According to his theory, when the vital force is insulted by mental, emotional, or physical stress, it responds with symptoms that are its attempts to restore equilibrium to the health of the individual. From this premise he deduced that in order for true healing to take place, it was necessary to give a remedy that mimicked the symptoms produced by the vital force.

So, for example, if someone has a cold, one symptom is a runny nose. This is understood to mean that the vital force is trying to rid the body of the virus and other toxins through this nasal discharge. A remedy would then be in order that would match all of the physical, mental, and emotional symptoms that the individual was exhibiting. This remedy in turn, would allow the vital force to continue the healing process in a safe, effective, and expedient manner that would provide a cure.

Allopathic medicine, *allo* – opposite, *pathy* – disease, which is what is currently practiced by the majority of physicians, runs directly contrary to the theory of homeopathy. In the same example, allopathic medicine would prescribe a decongestant to dry up the nasal congestion, which directly opposes the vital force's attempts to use this discharge as part of the healing process. In more serious symptom complexes, continual suppression of the vital force by treatment with allopathic medicine can lead to deeper and more serious levels of disease.

Until the early part of the twentieth century, homeopathy was the main field of medicine taught in most medical schools. The practice of allopathic medicine displaced it when pharmaceuticals became popular in the treatment of disease. Ironically, homeopathy is not even taught at the medical school in Philadelphia named after Hahnemann. However, it is highly popular in England and Prince Charles himself is an advocate of this important field of medicine. I have only scratched the surface in my discussion on this important topic and for those who want to know more about homeopathy, I suggest reading the excellent book written by George Vithoulkas, *The Science of Homeopathy.*

I was also fascinated by the other healing arts such as iridology, foot reflexology, and auricular therapy in acupuncture, all of which share the concept that the entire structure of body can be mapped out on, respectively, the iris, the sole of the foot, and the ear. This idea that the body is actually a hologram made sense to me since the DNA provided us at conception is identical in every cell of the body. The only reason why there is differentiation into the various tissues and organs is because certain genes are activated while others are suppressed. It seemed obvious to me that if the same DNA is in every cell, the entire body should be able to be mirrored on the iris, foot, ear, and even the tongue, which is used in traditional Chinese medicine as a way to assess the health and function of all the various organs.

I took an intriguing course on iridology with Dr. Bernard Jensen, the father of this art of healing. He was a dynamic man filled with vigor even though he was in his eighties when I met him. The history of iridology has its origin in Hungary when, in 1861, a young boy named Ignatz Peczely found an owl with a broken leg. He noticed a black stripe in the bird's iris and after nursing the leg back to health, he observed that this black stripe had been replaced with fine white lines. Years later when Peczely became a doctor, he began to realize that his patients had similar irregularities in their irises, depending on the type and stage of their illness. Over time he charted a map of the iris/body relationship.

Today, in order to more clearly see such structures and irregularities, a special camera is used to produce a magnified picture of the iris. Even without this magnification, one can tell general characteristics of a person's Chi or inner life force just by looking at the iris. For example, if all of the fibers are tightly interwoven, it means that the Chi is strong and that the person's underlying health is good. White exudates in the iris, most clearly seen in blue and green eyes, are indicative of toxicity in the body. I subsequently incorporated examination of the iris in my practice and found it to be useful in assessing the general health and well-being of my patients.

Dr. Jensen also recommended taking hot showers alternating with cold water which, he said, maintained good health because of the effect that this has on the skin. Most people don't know that the skin does more than just hold the outsides in. In fact, it is the largest organ of the body. One of its functions is to act as an excretory organ along with the intestinal tract and kidney. The application of cold water alternating with hot causes the pores of the skin to open and close, allowing the body to discharge toxins through the surface of the skin.

That is why in Sweden, home of the sauna, it is common for people to have their saunas outside surrounded by snow, giving them the opportunity to put this theory into action. After sitting in the sauna for fifteen to twenty minutes, they then roll around in the snow and quickly go back into the sauna again. This may be the secret behind their beautiful skin.

For over twenty years, I have followed Dr. Jensen's advice, even during the freezing cold winters when I was living in Minnesota. As a result, I have had significant health benefits. If nothing else, these showers absolutely wake me up on those mornings when I am having a hard time getting started!

I also enjoyed studying foot reflexology. As I received my foot reflexology treatments that involved massaging the sole of the foot in combination with the application of essential oils, I felt all of my anxiety and tension melt away and often ended up falling asleep. This therapy, every session of which produced such a state of profound relaxation for me, was useful in reducing the stress that had made me vulnerable to depression.

Later on, when I joined a multispecialty holistic center that had massage therapists on staff, I also learned that emotional trauma is stored in the fascia, or connective tissue between muscles. During a massage, it was common for women who had suppressed memories of being sexually abused, to suddenly break down in tears as these disturbing memories were released from their tissues. Fortunately, we also had psychotherapists on staff and when this happened, we immediately referred these patients to them.

The healing action of essential oils, also useful in massage, has a long, rich history dating back to the time of Egyptians. The olfactory nerve connects to other parts of the brain, including the limbic system, which controls emotions, making these essential oils a safe and effective addition to the treatment of depression and anxiety. Certain oils such as lavender and patchouli have a particularly calming, healing effect. I have used these myself to help improve my mood and sense of well-being.

Each oil has its own specific beneficial effects. Eucalyptus can be highly effective in treating upper respiratory infections and peppermint oil is useful in treating a wide variety of gastrointestinal disorders. I also went to a conference in which a medical doctor, who was lecturing on the use of essential oils in his practice, stated that by using the essential oil *ylang-ylang* in the treatment of hypertensive patients, he noted a significant reduction in their blood pressure. In order to get the maximum benefit from each oil, it is important that each one be natural and not synthetic. *The Complete Book of Essential Oils and Aromatherapy* by Valerie Ann Wordwood is an excellent text for those who want to learn more about this field.

Bach flower remedies are another safe modality in the treatment of mild to moderate depression and other emotional disorders. Dr. Edward Bach (1886-1936) developed a specialized branch of herbal medicine employing flowers that were distilled into a liquid and administered in drop form. Through observation and testing, he found that these remedies were useful in the treatment of specific emotional imbalances. I have used these remedies in the early stages of my depressive episodes and found them effective in improving my mood and preventing me from spiraling into deeper levels of despair and despondency.

For those who want to learn more about this topic, a good reference source is *The Bach Flower Remedies.* This is a compilation of three books by Dr. Bach and Dr. F.J. Wheeler. I highly recommend that one take these Bach flower remedies and/or essential oils under the supervision of a healthcare provider who is knowledgeable in the use of these modalities.

* * * * *

Continued exposure to the lessons and books issued by the church fueled my interest in a study group where the various topics that I was reading were being discussed. It was there that I met Anthony, the leader of the group, who would become a dear friend and a pillar of support for me. In the years that followed he would always be there to help guide me through my darkest hours of trials and tribulations.

There was also a teaching center in New York City where prayer services and lectures were held on Saturday nights and Sundays mornings. My wife did not want me to attend these services, still threatened by my decision to step outside of the Jewish religion despite the fact that I explained to her that I had started down on a path that was important to me and I did not want to walk away from it. Sadly, we found it impossible to work out a compromise with the result that she filed for divorce while I was in the last year of my residency.

At the time of our break-up, my wife was so threatened by my spiritual beliefs that the divorce agreement contained a clause stating that I would "not do anything to attempt to convert our child from Judaism or encourage her in any way to abandon the Jewish faith," even though I continued to explain that my desire to follow my new path was not a rejection of the Jewish faith. Judaism contained some valuable truths for me, but I believed that it was only part of the spectrum of spiritual knowledge. I had no plans to try to convert my child. I just wanted to have the option to share with Staci concepts outside of the world of Judaism. As far as I was concerned, she would always be free to follow her heart and live her life according to her own choices.

Staci was three years old at the time of the divorce, and I felt that my wife was always going to make it difficult for me to be with my daughter. It seemed clear to me based on what was written in the divorce decree, that she was trying to build a wall of fear and distrust that would separate me from my child, a wall that would be there until Staci was old enough to see the truth for herself. I decided that in order to pursue my spiritual aspirations, I needed to study with my teacher, a remarkable individual, who was the head of the church. With a heavy heart, I kissed my daughter good-bye, a decision I would later come to deeply regret, and left for church headquarters in California. I prayed that one day Staci would understand why I had to leave.

My mother was even more incensed than my wife about the reasons why I had decided to move to California. Mom had an incredible amount of pride in her Jewish heritage and I was excoriated for my attempts to think outside of the box of this religion. She even went so far as to suggest that I become an Orthodox Jew in order to satisfy my desire to explore new realms of religious philosophy. The irony underlying her desperate need to keep me under the wings of Judaism was that she was an atheist. When I confronted her with this paradox, she replied, “So what? There is a whole sect of Jews that don’t believe in God!” My father kept silent, although his anger was clearly reflected in his eyes.

Mom searched her soul, looking for what she did wrong that would have caused her son to be attracted to what she considered to be a “New Age cult.” She concluded, God bless her, that my “warped” thinking was due to the fact that, in my youth, I had watched too many episodes of *The Twilight Zone* and *The Outer Limits* as well as other science fiction programs on TV. As soon as I heard this, I knew that there was no way I could ever explain to her why I was taking a new road in life.

I made the trip across the country in early 1984, with the faith that I would find some employment opportunity in California. Soon after arriving there, I did meet with a professional placement counselor who put me in touch with a group of primary care physicians that were looking for a family doctor to man their new satellite office in Newbury Park, which wasn't too far from where the church was located. Since the clinic was fully equipped with an X-ray machine and all the bells and whistles that I would need to run a very efficient medical office, I eagerly looked forward to building my practice.

The headquarters of the church were located on the grounds of the former Gillette estate. Here was a magnificent chapel where services were held four times a week, a Montessori school, and a school called Summit University that offered classes in many spiritual topics to people who came from all over the world to attend these courses. There were also offices for the staff and a large cafeteria where lunch was served after Sunday services. And there was even a swimming pool in the shape of a razor blade in honor of the former owners.

It was in the chapel that I saw my teacher in person for the first time. I had seen her on video on numerous occasions, but the moment she stepped up to the podium was electrifying, a moment that is indelibly etched in my memory. She had crystal clear green eyes that were filled with compassion and seemed to look directly into my heart and soul. Her dark brown hair was tastefully coiffed and her face was graced with high cheekbones and a smile that promised joy and happiness. Although petite, she radiated an aura of power, strength, and intensity that were reflected in her lectures, which provided profound insights into the mysteries and wonders of all the world's major religions and were delivered in a voice that commanded attention.

The church also held quarterly conferences that were attended by individuals from all over the country. It was at one of these conferences that I would meet my next wife. I was sitting in the chapel and next to me was one of the few remaining empty seats. As the service was about to get under way, a beautiful young woman whom I had never met before, sat down hurriedly in this seat. When our eyes met, my heart soared like an eagle. I tingled all over.

Later on we spoke and Mary told me that she felt the same way about me. After the conference concluded, we had the chance to spend a few days together. She was from Massachusetts and was taking a break from her career as a dancer in order to attend Summit University. One night, as we walked along the beach in Malibu, professing our love for each other, we saw a shooting star, which we took as a sign of heaven's approval of our union. On our third date, I proposed to her and she happily accepted. Even though I had just been divorced from my wife for a few months, I was eager to get married again.

We soon married and moved to Agoura Hills, which was closer to my office. There were many advantages for me as I made the transition from my residency program into private practice. My hours were much more reasonable and I was on call only once a week. There was also an increase in my salary that went a long way in helping me pay for my alimony and child support payments. I also enjoyed the autonomy and freedom that went along with having my own office.

I did, however, have to make a major adjustment in this new practice: dealing with HMOs and all the guidelines that went along with managed care. During my residency program, I was free to order any diagnostic test or procedure that I thought the patient needed without having to get permission from any insurance company or third-party payer. However, the managed care movement – and its control of patient care – was just getting started in California. Each time I wanted to refer a patient to a specialist or order an expensive diagnostic test such as a CAT scan, my request would first have to be approved by the insurance company, which, in my opinion, handcuffed my ability to practice medicine efficiently. But by the time I adjusted to having to deal with this vexing issue, it was time to leave California because the church would soon be moving to Big Sky Country.

Chapter Four

As it turned out, the church was moving to Corwin Springs, Montana, after purchasing the Malcolm Forbes Ranch, which was located just outside of Yellowstone Park. This property was renamed The Royal Teton Ranch in honor of the spectacular Grand Teton Mountains located in nearby Jackson Hole, Wyoming.

The goal was to have a self-sufficient spiritual community in the wilderness, away from the craziness and crowds of Southern California. Both my wife and I were thrilled with the idea of moving to Montana and being part of this community. Unfortunately, job opportunities were scarce in that part of the country and, since I needed a steady income, we couldn't relocate there, although we did plan to make Montana our home as soon as it became financially feasible. Meanwhile, as a fallback plan, we decided to look into employment opportunities in the Minneapolis/St. Paul area where the church had two teaching centers.

A good opportunity did open up for me in the St. Paul area where a hospital was looking for another physician to take over the practice of a retired doctor, offering an attractive package that included a guaranteed salary for two years and health and vacation benefits as well as paying for our move to St. Paul. This was an offer that I couldn't refuse. So we packed up our bags and, in late fall of 1987, we left for Minnesota.

Initially, we moved into an apartment in the St. Louis Park area and attended services on a regular basis at the teaching center in Minneapolis. This was a beautiful, stately mansion that was located on the banks of a large lake and housed about thirty staff members. We became friendly with the head of the center who offered us the position of running the other center in St. Paul. My wife and I were delighted to have this opportunity and immediately moved into these headquarters, which was a smaller house that we shared with ten other staff members. There, I lived the sort of monastic lifestyle that I relished, rising every morning at five for a two-hour prayer service and then, after a full days work at the office, attending an evening prayer service from seven to nine.

I loved living in the Twin Cities. Yes, it was EXTREMELY cold in the winter. The natives joked, "Minnesota has two seasons, winter's here and winter's gone." But the resilient inhabitants of this area, many of whom were of Scandinavian descent, took advantage of the winter by participating in such sports as ice fishing and cross country skiing. Minneapolis, also known as the "Mini-Apple," provided similar cultural events and fine dining that was available in the Big Apple, while St. Paul was more provincial and charming.

As I continued to enjoy our new life in Minnesota, I realized that I had inherited a practice that, before having been purchased by the hospital had been inactive for a long time and as a result attracted few patients. I tried to resuscitate the practice by becoming more active in the community, joining the Rotary Club, etc. But after a while, it became apparent that the practice was beyond repair and it was time to move on to another practice opportunity in the Twin Cities. I departed with the blessings of the hospital administrator. Soon after leaving, I contacted another placement counselor who put me in touch with a multispecialty group that was looking for a family doctor to join their practice. I met with all of the physicians in the group and found them to be friendly and pleasant individuals. After my interview, they graciously welcomed me into their group.

However, my wife and I still shared the dream of moving to the church headquarters in Montana as soon as it was practical. By this time, she had graduated from nursing school. Since there was a need for nurses in the healing center at the ranch, we decided that she would make the move first. I would join her when I found a viable employment opportunity within driving distance of headquarters We had a tearful parting although I knew in my heart that I would soon be joining her.

After she left, I moved into the larger teaching center in Minneapolis, sharing a small room, just big enough to squeeze in bunk beds, with a friend who was a surgeon and had just moved to the Twin Cities. This man also shared my devotion to the spiritual path, a factor that more than compensated for our humble living conditions. It was fortuitous that my medical group was looking for a surgeon to join their practice. I recommended my friend for this position and they were happy to have him.

In my desire to serve my fellow housemates, I volunteered to do the produce shopping for the thirty staff members who lived at the center. During my days off, I would fast and go to the grocery store where I filled two carts with bushels of carrots, broccoli, kale, collards, and a variety of other vegetables. Arriving home, I pushed myself to the limit by preparing dinner for everyone, which was followed by a two-hour prayer service. I felt like I was a battle-hardened spiritual warrior ready for any challenge.

Many months would pass but finally an opportunity for employment in Big Sky Country became available. An urgent care center in Billings, Montana, which was a three-hour drive from the ranch, was looking for a part-time doctor. I was able to work out an arrangement whereby I would work three consecutive twelve-hour shifts that would give me four days off to spend at church headquarters. They were pleased to have me join them and the feeling was mutual. So, I left Minneapolis in the summer of 1989 and was on the road again, traveling to the Royal Teton Ranch. I had no idea that my dream of living in a spiritual community that was in a part of the country that I considered to be the closest to paradise on earth, would turn into a nightmare not too long after I arrived there.

* * * * *

The Royal Teton Ranch was surrounded by thousands of acres of wilderness and cradled by the Gallatin Mountains. The staff resided in trailers and the medical department consisted of cabins across the street from the ranch. It was necessary to have some type of a public relations endeavor with our neighbors because most of them believed that we were a cult due to our "radical religious beliefs." In order to foster goodwill, the church ran a restaurant that was well patronized by the locals, no doubt because of the excellent food that was prepared there.

A steep path led up to the chapel. Beyond that was a spiraling, rocky road that swirled around the mountainous terrain leading to a place called the Heart of the Inner Retreat. This area was surrounded by a never-ending forest of pine trees, which stood like proud sentinels on the majestic mountain peaks. Each time I was there and inhaled the crisp, rarefied air, my entire being was filled with an overwhelming sense of peace, serenity, and freedom. I felt like I was finally "home." It was here that the summer conferences were held, as people from all over the world came to gather under tents in the wilderness, just like the tribes of Israel in ancient times past, to pray and hear the teachings of our spiritual leader.

My wife and I shared a trailer with other staff members. Our modest living accommodations consisted of a small room that barely fit our bed and dresser. I was more than willing to give up the worldly comforts in order to live in this spiritual community that was surrounded by the peace and splendor of nature.

I also enjoyed the three days a week that I worked with the staff at the urgent care center in Billings. They were cordial and made me feel at home in my new place of employment. My work there provided enough money to pay for the alimony and child support, a high priority for me.

I rented a sparsely furnished apartment near the center, but after those three days were up, I always looked forward to making the trip back to the ranch. Each time I left the plains of Billings, I became energized by the sight of the mountains that welcomed me back. As I made the approach to my new home, my gaze was always held captive by the beauty of the landscape that was dotted with elk, deer, bison, and other magnificent creatures.

I loved attending services in the beautiful chapel that was set up at the ranch and living with other devotees who all shared the common goal of building a community based on peace and brotherhood. I planned on spending the rest of my life there. Sadly, this was not to be.

The first step that would eventually lead to pandemonium at the ranch started in early 1990 when our teacher began to focus on the dire prophecies of the sixteenth century clairvoyant Nostradamus as well as those of Mother Mary and also the passages contained in Revelations, all of which predicted imminent world cataclysm and chaos. We were told to immediately make all preparations necessary into order to survive the bedlam that awaited us. It seems ludicrous in hindsight that I believed these shocking predictions. But the spiritual teachings and insights that I had received from this charismatic woman had touched the deepest parts of my soul and were so profound that I turned a blind eye and participated in the madness that was to come.

The church went into a full-scale survival mode and these preparations were emotionally, mentally, and physically draining for me. Due to the increased demands of my work schedule at the ranch, I did not have time to go to my job in Billings. Because of my prolonged absences there, they had no other choice but to let me go. Then, for some unexplained reason, after three months of intense preparations, the threat of these ominous predictions faded away and everything was back to "normal" at the church. However, life was anything but back to normal for me.

I was dazed and confused. I did not understand why these dire predictions, which were given with such certainty by my teacher, never came to pass. My trust and faith in her was shattered. Shell-shocked and worn to a frazzle from the arduous preparations of the last few months, I wandered aimlessly on the fields and valleys surrounding the ranch. With no source of income, my sanity finally cracked after I received a letter from my ex-wife's attorney threatening me with legal action on the grounds of having missed one alimony/child support payment. In desperation, I insisted that Mary, despite her protests, accompany me in returning to my parents' home in New York. I had a vain hope that they would welcome me with open arms and give me the comfort and support that I so badly needed.

We landed on their doorstep in the middle of the night in March 1990. Instead of the warm reception that I hoped for, we received a cold greeting from my parents. It froze me to the core. It was clear that my parents were still vehemently against the church, my move to Montana, and my participation in the incredulous survival plans undertaken at the ranch. The anger that they directed at me only intensified my emotional anguish.

My wife, whose priority was to remain in Montana, was unhappy that I had dragged her to New York. My parents gave her money for the airfare to return to Montana and made no secret of being happy to see her go. As for me, I was too numb to care about her departure. Now that I was at home, I desperately wanted to visit Staci, but since she was only nine years old at the time, I did not contact her because I didn't want her to see me in my frayed emotional state.

Since I had no money to meet my financial obligations, my parents grudgingly paid my bills. I was grateful for their help. However, after a few weeks of growing impatient with my idleness, my mother called the New York State Medical Board and single-handedly got the board to renew my expired medical license. Mom was a force to be reckoned with.

Now that I was once again a licensed physician in the state of New York, my parents insisted that I get a job. Since my car was in Montana, they drove me to my interviews for various employment opportunities, including one at the largest HMOs in the metropolitan region. This entire experience was nothing but unrelenting misery for me. I felt suffocated by the crowded, concrete jungle of New York City. My soul needed to be surrounded by nature in order to thrive.

Feeling cut off from my spiritual roots weighed heavily on my heart, but the anguish that was wracking my soul intensified a thousandfold when I was served with divorce papers from my wife in Montana. She had grown impatient with the slow pace of my recovery and was anxious to get on with her life. Determined to not let this send me into deeper depths of depression, I resolved to fight back and free myself from the gloom that was engulfing me.

My first course of action was to embark upon an exercise program. After each workout session, I felt the emotional and physical toxins that had built up within me melt away. Research has shown that exercise can be an effective tool in the treatment in depression, and a recent study by the University of Texas at Austin revealed that even one exercise session can have an immediate improvement in mood. This definitely worked for me, and I wholeheartedly recommend exercise as an adjunct to the treatment of depression.

As the weeks passed, the joy and optimism that I had been sorely lacking, returned to my world. I found myself eager to rejoin the spiritual community that I had left behind in the Twin Cities. I also thirsted to be surrounded by the lakes and beauty in this part of the country. I called my professional placement counselor in Minnesota and he put me in touch with a physician that I knew in St. Paul who was looking for another doctor to join his practice. Since we had always had a good rapport, he was more than happy to have me join his practice. We made our agreement over the phone, and within a week I had packed my bags and was prepared to leave.

My parents, who had indicated their willingness to forgive my debt, were extremely upset because they had assumed that I was now going to permanently reside in New York When they found out that I was determined to return to the Minneapolis-St. Paul area, they demanded all of their money back. Who could blame them? I did comply with their wishes and thanked them for all the help that they had given me. In September 1990, I made my way back to the Twin Cities, full of joy and hope not knowing that within eighteen months, I would descend into a world of insanity and self-destruction.

* * * * *

I arrived in the Twin Cities eager to start my new life, filled with so much excitement that my whole being felt electrified. The world before me sparkled with vibrant colors that bounced off the thickly leaved trees and the many lakes that decorated the landscape. In my energized state, I found that I did not need as much sleep, awaking refreshed each morning, hours before my alarm clock was set to go off. Although I did not know it at the time, my increased energy and euphoric mood were symptoms of the hypomania associated with my Bipolar 2 Disorder. However, since these feelings only enhanced my enjoyment of life without causing me any problems, I did not seek any help.

Meanwhile, the physician, whose partner I had become, was a friendly, easygoing man around my age with a unique sense of humor. For example, he reinforced my idea that ties were probably invented by a woman who wanted to get back at the man who had invented the torture device known as a brassiere. I agreed with him since each time I put on a tie, it felt as if I had a noose around my neck that was slowly choking me to death.

He said that he never wore ties because of safety

concerns. After seeing the puzzled look in my eyes, he gave me a vivid demonstration of the dangers associated with this article of clothing by grabbing hold of my tie and pulling me close to him, explaining that this action could be taken by any disgruntled patient. I assumed that he was kidding, but from that day forward, I never again wore a tie to the office.

In the summer of 1991, I attended a conference in California and it was here that my path would cross with that of wife number three. I had been divorced for about a year and a half and was enjoying my new life when I was introduced to a remarkable woman with sparkling blue eyes and a radiant smile that was warm and welcoming. Amy was also a physician, recently divorced with two young children and had been practicing alternative medicine in Connecticut for a number of years. Her interest and experience in this field of medicine intrigued me. The fact that we shared similar spiritual aspirations also drew me to her. We spent the next three days together and it didn't take long for sparks to start flying.

After returning to our respective practices, we conversed long distance daily, professing our love and devotion to each other. At the end of the summer, I spent a few days with her in Cape Cod, walking the beaches hand in hand, falling more and more in love. History repeated itself for me when, after a brief romance, we became engaged at the beginning of September with plans to marry in February 1992. I was also excited to hear that she and a holistic dentist were opening a healing center in January and were looking for an acupuncturist, a naturopath, psychotherapist, and massage therapist to join the group.

When I learned that my fiancée wanted us to work together as partners, I felt as though my prayers had been answered. My dream of working in a multispecialty holistic healing center was finally coming true. I was also thrilled with the idea of living closer to Staci. Once I moved back to Connecticut, I would be able to see her on a regular basis. I knew that it would take time and patience to rebuild our relationship after my being out of her life for so long, but I was grateful for the opportunity.

It seemed that this story was going to have a fairy tale ending with everybody living happily ever after, but soon I would be awakened from this blissful dream. In truth, Amy and I never had the chance to get to know each other during our brisk courtship. The stress of working and living together, combined with the added strain of adjusting to life with her two young children, would poison our relationship and lead to my next episode of suicidal depression.

I returned to my practice in Minnesota and told my colleague about my story of romance and plans of moving to Connecticut early next year. I was so blinded by my infatuated state that I assumed that he would share in my joy. But understandably enough he did not because from his point of view, my departure would only disrupt his practice. Looking back, I am sure that he questioned the sanity of my impetuous decision. However, he never expressed that thought and was gracious in allowing me to work with him until I was ready to go.

* * * * *

I moved to Connecticut in January 1992. Amy and I feverishly began to make wedding plans. Finally, the big day arrived. It did not, however, take long after we were married for problems to surface. In our brief but intense courtship, my wife had created in her mind the fantasy of me being her knight in shining armor, perfect in every way, sent to rescue her from the burdens that she carried. In reality, I had foibles like anyone else, and when she saw the "chinks" in my armor, her disappointment pierced my heart. I had given up everything for this woman – my home, my practice, my peaceful life in Minnesota – because I wanted to spend the rest of my life with her and now this dream seemed to be falling apart. Despite my "imperfections" she was still willing to do whatever it took to make our marriage work. So was I.

The realities of life however would begin to rock the tenuous foundations of our relationship almost immediately after we returned home from our honeymoon. Our new life together took on a schizophrenic quality. During the two weeks that her kids lived with their father, we lived like newlyweds. We had the freedom to enjoy the simple pleasures of life without the demands of children. However, upon the arrival of her kids for their two-week stay with us, our privacy evaporated. Chaos reigned. There was constant bickering between brother and sister that shattered any semblance of peace for me.

I also began to feel jealous and insecure because of the constant attention that my wife was devoting to her children. The wounds of my own inner child would have to heal before I could be free of any envy that prevented me from enjoying the company of her children. But I would have to hit bottom before this healing could begin.

My insecurity also carried over to my professional life. I began to question my ability to master the field of holistic medicine. Although I had studied alternative medicine over the years, I did not have many opportunities to use it with my patients. I felt overwhelmed by all the knowledge that I needed to incorporate into my new practice of medicine. Now the ghosts of doubt and fear that had haunted me in medical school returned to drive me down the same self-destructive path.

My self-esteem and sense of self-worth were then completely shattered when, after a month of marriage, my wife told me that I was not the man she thought I was. This rejection from a woman whom I had tried to please, tried to love in so many ways, ripped off the scab of a still unhealed memory buried deeply in my subconscious: the painful memory of an innocent child who craved his mother's love and strove unceasingly to obtain it, but was frequently rebuffed.

The demons of hell were now tugging at my ankles as they tried to drag me down into the depths of their dark, dank underworld. This familiar sensation chilled me to the marrow. Past experience had taught me that once I was in their grips, there would be no escape. I cried out silently for help, but my anguished pleas were muffled as I was pulled further down into the blackness of darkness.

I began to hate myself. Each time I looked in the mirror, I saw the reflection of a hideous beast. My mastery over sleep began to crumble when I started to awaken in the middle of the night, forced to lie in bed for hours dreading the arrival of daybreak. This was soon followed by nights that brought no sleep at all, leaving me in a disoriented and confused state. The simple tasks of writing a check or taking a shower became events of monumental proportions. My mind, usually clear, incisive, and analytical was my most prized possession and when it began to dissolve, an overwhelming fear gripped hold of me. It has been said that a mind is a terrible thing to waste, but for me, my mind was a terrible thing to lose.

The closest that I can come to describing this state of complete mental disarray is to compare it to the effects that alcohol has on the brain. The state of inebriation produces the same mental confusion and chaos that I was experiencing without any of the pleasant or relaxing effects afforded by this beverage. Interestingly, a recent study on sleep-deprived medical residents revealed that their blood alcohol levels were slightly above the normal legal limits. Lack of sleep increases the body's production of alcohol, which explained the reason for my declining mental acuity.

Fortunately, as soon as Amy recognized my debilitated state, she no longer allowed me to see patients at the center. Instead, I was confined to my corner of the office, gazing blankly out the window, sinking deeper into a world of paranoia and anxiety. I remember once during this terrible time when two men in white uniforms had arrived at the office to do electrical repairs. In my deranged state, I hid in my room because I was convinced that they were orderlies from the psychiatric hospital who were going to put me in a straightjacket and take me away.

I was also wrapped in a choking cloak of anxiety. My solar plexus felt as though it was tied up in knots, making it difficult for me to breathe. I could not sit still as this anxiety devoured me from the inside out, making every second of every minute cruel and unrelenting torture.

As I retreated into the role of a helpless, frightened child, my wife took more and more control of my life. Finally, at the beginning of April, I became so incapacitated that she no longer allowed me to come to the office. Fearing for my safety, she hired a friend to stay with me while she was at work. Even though she was doing the best she could to help me, I felt intimidated by the power and control that she had over my life. In my demented state, she had become the wicked witch from the Land of Oz.

I came to feel like a prisoner, trapped in my own home. An instinct to escape overcame any rational judgment that I still possessed. As soon as the opportunity arose, I grabbed my car keys and made the harrowing ninety-minute drive to my parents' home. Their patience worn thin from my ongoing battle with depression, they made no secret that they were not happy to see me. In fact, to my dismay, they called Amy and told her to come pick me up. My irrational fear of my wife's wrath, augmented by the thought of returning to the home that I now considered my prison, drove me into an act of desperation and complete insanity.

Going into my parents' bedroom, I swung open their closet door, grabbed the first bottle of pills that I could find and chugged down in three seconds flat what turned out to be a prescription for muscle relaxants. My next memory was waking up completely disoriented on a stretcher in the emergency room. Ironically, this was the same hospital that my parents had taken me to when I had my first episode of depression almost twenty years earlier.

As soon as I had recovered sufficiently from this overdose, I was subjected to the harrowing experience of being transferred to the psychiatric unit of this hospital in the middle of the night. Patients were sleeping everywhere, even on the floor. I could not wait to get out. Fortunately, my wife, who was at our home in Connecticut, suggested that I be transferred to a psychiatric institute that was for healthcare professionals in Connecticut. She soon arrived to take me to this facility where I was evaluated by a psychiatrist who prescribed antidepressants.

In the early stages of the treatment program, I huddled in my room, lying curled up in my bed, leaving only for meals and mandatory therapy sessions. Hopelessness and despair were my constant companions. I was certain that my breakdown so early in our relationship would put an end to our marriage. I loved Amy and the thought of divorce was extremely painful for me. But when she came to visit several days later and said that she loved me and was still committed to our marriage, I was determined to do whatever I could to get better.

I began to take my first steps towards wellness by changing the lens that colored my perception of the world around me. Instead of focusing on feelings of gloom and doom, I turned my attention to all the gifts that Life was offering me. Happiness, love, abundance could all be mine if I made a conscious decision to allow them into my world. This thought brought me the first glimmer of hope. Day by day, I continued to focus on all that I had in my life instead of what I was lacking and as I did, my mood steadily improved. By the end of two weeks, my sense of joy, hope, and purpose had returned. In early May, I was ready for discharge.

Spring in all its radiance greeted me when I returned home. I was fully charged and awoke early every morning eagerly anticipating the start of each new day as my hypomanic symptoms once again presented themselves. But as before, since they only enhanced my enjoyment of life and caused no problems, they went undetected. My confidence and self-esteem were fully restored through my connection to God through prayer. Regular exercise was also integral to my recovery. I looked forward to mastering the field of alternative medicine and working with my colleagues. It was wonderful to be warmly welcomed back by everybody at the center.

In order to acquire the knowledge of holistic medicine necessary to start my practice, I sat in with my wife as she worked with her many patients. Amy was kind and loving. She took extra time to explain to me the whys and hows of her approach to treatment. I also continued to go to medical conferences, which covered in depth all the topics that I needed to include in my arsenal of treatment modalities. Before long, I started to build my practice from the overflow of patients waiting to see my wife. Integrating conventional with alternative medicine, I was passionate in my work and loved every minute of it.

In an effort to strengthen our bond and inject some playfulness into our marriage, we decided to take square dancing lessons. In order to maintain this atmosphere of loving harmony, I went to a psychotherapist to try to untangle the knots in my psychology that might have been contributing to the discord in our marriage. After listening to my story, the therapist thought that the best approach would be to work with my inner child.

In my sessions with her, I found out that the main driving force behind my pattern of rushing into relationships was coming from my inner child's cries for the unconditional love and nurturing that he had never received from his mother. Up until that time, I had never been conscious of this issue. Now that it had been brought out into the light, however, I actively took measures to be the parent to my inner child. Following my therapist's advice, I gathered pictures of myself as a child and spoke to him lovingly, as a father would to his son. I took those pictures everywhere I went so that I would be there for him whenever he needed me. I found this approach particularly useful to defuse the pangs of jealousy that plagued me whenever Amy showed her children affection.

After completing this therapy, I became more active in the lives of my wife's children and thoroughly enjoyed their company. Ultimately, a tight bond formed between us. I actually started to look forward to their two-week stay.

However, although this removed one thorn in the side of our marriage, Amy and I realized that we had rushed into this marriage and were not prepared to handle the burdens that each of us carried. As difficult as it was, we both decided that it would be best for us to divorce, but we parted on good terms and have remained friends to this day.

I was grateful to Amy for all that she had taught me, not only about holistic medicine, but also how to run a practice, consequently preparing me for the next step: opening my own office. There was another apparent blessing that came from the time that I spent at the center. I was introduced to a group of chiropractors who offered me an attractive employment opportunity that would provide me with the supplemental income that I needed as I started to build my new practice. At the time though, the possibility that this "blessing" might turn out to be a curse never crossed my mind.

Chapter Five

The Realtor I worked with when looking for a new office location mentioned a condominium complex only four miles down the road from my previous practice that was a mix of residential and professional offices. As soon as I saw the space and heard that the name of the complex was Harmony Place, I knew that this location was destined to be the home of my new practice.

I believe that harmony is one of the essential keys necessary for wellness. In my experience, without harmony, there is a natural tendency for our mental, emotional, and physical health to drift into a state of instability that ultimately leads to disease. In February of 1995, I opened the door to my new practice that I christened **Harmony Health Care**.

In order to avoid the sterile atmosphere of most medical offices, I created a relaxing, peaceful environment in which the healing would begin as soon as the patient walked through the door. The only downside to the office was that it was adjacent to a cemetery, which was not good *Feng Shui.* But I even used that to my advantage: teasing my patients by saying that they could either listen to my advice and become active participants in their quest for health or end up "next door."

I considered the relationship between my patients and me to be a partnership. I would provide them with all of my medical expertise and experience and it would be their decision to apply it. Many times I heard that they often felt rushed when they visited their doctor. In fact, more frequently than I had imagined, they didn't feel like their physician was really listening to what they were saying. In order to avoid this, I set aside ninety minutes for the initial office visit and thirty minutes for follow-up appointments.

Most of the patients who came to see me had a history of long-term, chronic health problems that were not responding to the treatment regimens other physicians had prescribed. The fact of the matter was that I needed this time in order to address all of their concerns. I started the visit by allowing them to take as much time as they needed to tell me their complete medical history, interrupting them only when necessary to ask a question.

The importance of paying careful attention to what patients are saying as they give their medical history cannot be understated. I learned this during my residency program when the attending physician who trained me said something that I would never forget: "Listen to the patient. They are telling you the diagnosis." The art of listening is also invaluable in enhancing the healing process. I remember one time when, after an initial office visit, a patient said to me, "I don't know what you did, but I feel better already." Ironically, all I had done was listen.

I realized that the treatment recommendations that I offered most patients could be daunting because these often involved significant lifestyle changes including revamping their diets, taking nutritional supplements, exercising according to individual preference and capacity, and, most importantly, addressing the underlying emotional imbalances that were at the root cause of their illness. I empathized with them because I had made many of the changes in my life that I recommended to them and knew how challenging it could be. For support, I tried to make it easier for them to make this transition by offering them written material that covered all of the topics that I discussed as well as a form that listed all of the recommended supplements with clear instructions on how to take them along with an explanation of the purpose of each supplement. I also took the time to answer all of their questions and tried to return their phone calls on a timely basis.

In my practice, many patients presented with depression as one of their symptoms, but usually their mood disturbance was associated with a constellation of other symptoms and rarely occurred in a vacuum. Common symptoms associated with their depressed mood included fatigue, muscle aches and pains, weight gain, difficulty concentrating, poor memory, decreased libido, cold intolerance, hair loss, digestive disturbances, and more. I learned that many physicians had attributed these symptoms as being only psychosomatic in origin and secondary to the depression, which meant that instead of investigating the etiology of the symptom complex, they would only prescribe an antidepressant.

That is not to say that medications do not have a role in the treatment of mental illness. However, during my years in practice, I frequently found that an underlying disease process, often ignored or not recognized by the medical establishment, had either caused or exacerbated their depression. If these diseases were diagnosed and the appropriate treatment was instituted, patients often experienced dramatic relief of their depression without the use of antidepressants. These illnesses include: subclinical hypothyroidism, candidiaisis, and brain allergies.

I feel strongly that more information should be given on these three illnesses because, in my experience, many people who have these conditions as the underlying cause of their depression are not getting the care that is needed to treat their illness. I will provide a brief explanation of each condition along with examples of patients who had these illnesses in order to illustrate the marked improvement in their mental, emotional, and physical health once they were properly diagnosed and treated.

First, let us consider **subclinical hypothyroidism**, a disease in which the thyroid is underactive. As a result of this dysfunction, an individual can present with depression and many of its associated symptoms, including fatigue, poor memory and concentration, weight gain, difficulty losing weight, low libido, constipation, muscle aches and pains, cold intolerance, dry skin, and hair loss. The term subclinical refers to the fact that, in the face of these symptoms, the thyroid blood tests are normal. If this is the case, most physicians will not treat for an underactive thyroid because they use the blood tests as the sole parameter in the diagnosis of hypothyroidism.

I had found though, based on the training that I had received, together with my clinical experience, that the thyroid blood tests are not always accurate in the diagnosis of hypothyroidism, for several reasons. First of all, since the levels of thyroid hormones like most hormones fluctuate throughout the day, a single blood test is not always an adequate measurement. Secondly, the reference range given for levels of thyroid hormones is not always reliable in making the diagnosis of hypothyroidism.

Finally, these blood tests don't take into account the existence of the syndrome known as thyroid hormone resistance. This means that the receptors for thyroid hormone that activate the cell do not respond to normal levels of thyroid hormone, so higher levels are needed to overcome this resistance and treat the symptoms of hypothyroidism. Insulin resistance – as seen in diabetes in which increasing doses of this hormone are needed to maintain normal levels of blood sugar – is recognized and treated by the medical community, yet most physicians have not embraced the concept of thyroid hormone resistance.

It is important to get blood tests in diagnosing thyroid dysfunction, but since they are not always accurate, it begs the question as to what other diagnostic modalities are available to detect this condition. The most important tool in the diagnosis of hypothyroidism is the clinical history of the patient, making it all the more important to listen because often he or she is giving you the diagnosis. If a patient presents with most of the symptoms associated with hypothyroidism, there is a high index of suspicion that this person is hypothyroid, even in the presence of normal thyroid blood tests.

The basal body temperature, which is the temperature

that is measured before the patient gets out of bed in the morning, is also a valuable test in assessing thyroid function. That is because the thyroid, through its effects on metabolism, heats the body. If thyroid function is low, then in turn the basal body temperature will be low. Dr. Broda Barnes, an endocrinologist and pioneer in the field of subclinical hypothyroidism clearly recounts in his book: *Hypothyroidism: The Unsuspected Illness*, the effectiveness of the basal body temperature as one of the parameters in the diagnosis of this illness. *The Broda O. Barnes Research Foundation* is a great resource for information on subclinical hypothyroidism. This organization can be contacted at the following Web site: *http://www.brodabarnes.org.* Another excellent book that I recommend for those who want to know more about this topic is *Solved: The Riddle of Illness* by Stephen Langer, M.D.

In addition to the use of basal body temperature as one parameter used in the diagnosis of this thyroid disorder, there is also a twenty-four-hour urine test that measures levels of thyroid hormones. Although the medical profession uses twenty-four-hour urine tests as a diagnostic tool for many illnesses, it is not recognized as a valid test for the diagnosis of thyroid disease. But in my years of practice, it was a valuable adjunctive tool in the diagnosis of hypothyroidism.

In my clinical experience, I also found, along with other physicians in the field of integrative medicine, that Armour® thyroid, a natural form of thyroid, was often far superior to Synthroid®, which as the name implies, is a synthetic form of thyroid and is prescribed by most physicians for the treatment of hypothyroidism. One reason for this is the fact that the hormones contained in Armour® thyroid, unlike Synthroid®, are structurally similar to the thyroid hormones produced by the body, which greatly enhances the efficacy of this medication. In addition, Armour® has both forms of thyroid hormone that are needed in the treatment of hypothyroidism whereas Synthroid® has only one. Although the medical community in general frowns on the use of Armour® thyroid in the treatment of hypothyroidism, in my practice I encountered many patients who were not responding to Synthroid® and when I started them on Armour® thyroid, their health improved dramatically.

One example of a patient who presented to me with a history of depression clearly stands out in my mind. Melanie was a forty-eight-year-old woman who several months before seeing me had been hospitalized for major depression. She was told that she had a "chemical imbalance" and had been started on Prozac® with only minimal success. When I saw her in my office, in addition to being depressed, she presented with other symptoms including weight loss, anxiety, fatigue, difficulty concentrating, and cold intolerance. She was unable to work and was on disability as a result of her depression. I did a thorough medical history, physical exam, and laboratory tests including a twenty-four-hour urine test for thyroid and adrenal hormones and reviewed her basal body temperature.

Although Melanie had normal thyroid blood tests, I found, based on her history, twenty-four-hour urine test, and low basal body temperature that she had subclinical hypothyroidism, as well as decreased adrenal function and low levels of the female hormone progesterone. After treating her for a month with Armour® thyroid, progesterone, and other natural or bio-identical hormones as well as nutritional supplements, she had a marked improvement in her symptoms and was able to return to work part time. And after two months of treatment, she was feeling completely better and was able to return to work full time. In the years that she was under my care, she never had a relapse of her depression and continued to do extremely well.

Another illness that can present with the symptoms of depression is a condition known as **candidiasis,** which refers to the overgrowth of yeast in the intestinal tract that is commonly caused by antibiotics, birth control pills, alcohol, and a diet that is high in sugar. The yeast produce organic acids, which can be measured in a twenty-four-hour urine test. These organisms also produce mycotoxins that along with the organic acids, directly affect the brain and can cause depression as well as poor memory and concentration, fatigue, and mood swings. In addition, this overgrowth of yeast can cause a variety of gastrointestinal symptoms, including gas, bloating, abdominal cramping, and diarrhea.

Recurrent courses of antibiotics are the most common cause of this condition because they kill not only the "bad" bacteria, but the good as well, known as Lactobacillus acidophilus, the same bacteria found in yogurt. These bacteria live in the intestinal tract and are vital to good health because they make vitamins, improve immune system function, enhance bowel function, and reduce the growth of yeast. Treatment of this illness, which includes dietary changes, antifungals (both herbal and/or prescription), and replacement of the acidophilus, can significantly improve mood, memory, and concentration, as well as the intestinal symptoms, without the need for antidepressants.

Lynn was a patient whose life was turned around after the diagnosis and treatment of this disease. A thirty-four-year-old woman and mother of four, she had been throughout most of her life on recurrent courses of antibiotics for the treatment of chronic sinus infections. By the time she came to see me, Lynn was at the end of her rope. She stated that she was "shutting down," as she put it, both mentally and emotionally, plagued by chronic fatigue and recurrent episodes of abdominal pain. Standard diagnostic tests done by her physician were all normal. After taking a detailed medical history, doing a physical exam, and reviewing the results of blood and stool tests that showed the overgrowth of yeast, I diagnosed her with candidiasis and recommended the treatment protocol mentioned previously. Within one month, in her own words, her "life was worth living again" and as each month went by her health continued to improve. It was a very satisfying experience to have been able to help this woman who had been suffering for so long, barely surviving, but certainly not thriving. For more information on this topic, I recommend the book *The Yeast Connection* by William Crook, M.D.

The medical profession though, has several misconceptions regarding the diagnosis or even the existence of chronic candidiaisis. First, the majority of doctors claim that yeast normally occur in the intestinal tract and therefore should not be considered pathogenic, or capable of causing disease. While this is true, they fail to take into account that it is the *overgrowth* of yeast that triggers depression and its associated symptoms. The medical community also maintains that there are no valid tests to detect candidiaisis, which is another fallacy since certain labs offer specialized blood and urine tests as well as stool cultures that are helpful in making the diagnosis of this illness. As importantly, they ignore the fact that a thorough clinical history and physical examination can also lead to the diagnosis of this illness.

Another condition associated with depression is a syndrome known as **brain allergies.** In this situation, antibodies in the bloodstream interact with both food and environmental allergens. This interaction causes the release of histamine and other compounds that directly affect the brain and produce a wide range of symptoms, including depression, mood swings, poor memory, difficulty concentrating, fatigue, and many more. Specialized tests are needed to detect the presence of these antibodies, known as IgG, but most physicians in their workup for allergies solely order tests that measure for IgE antibodies that trigger only the common symptoms associated with allergies. These include sneezing, itchy eyes, and nasal congestion. As a result, many of the allergens that cause the brain dysfunctions noted above go undetected. The diagnosis and treatment of these allergens can have dramatic results.

A ten-year-old boy named Jake who had a Jekyll-Hyde personality comes to mind in this regard. One minute he would be sweet and then the next he would turn into a monster. The bruises and bite marks on his mother's arms were testimony to the consequences of his destructive behavior. After the outburst subsided, he would become extremely remorseful and depressed. He was on antidepressants when he came to see me, but they weren't helping. In school, Jake was in a class for kids with special needs and was receiving poor grades.

There is one day that I will never forget. He was being tested for allergies to tomatoes. Before the test, Jake was subdued and calm but minutes after injecting him subdermally with a diluted dose of this substance, chaos broke out. "When I'm older," he screamed, literally foaming at the mouth, "I'm gonna come back and murder all of you!" It took four adults to restrain him and, thankfully, he calmed down dramatically right after we treated him for this allergen.

After identifying and then treating all of his allergens, Jake was a changed boy. He no longer had the destructive temper tantrums and his depression vanished. The bruises and bite marks on his mother's arms resolved, never to return again. He became a happy-go-lucky kid, doing so well in school that he was mainstreamed into the classes with his peers. After he completed treatment, his mother said something to me that I will never forget, "I prayed to God that He would give me my child back. Thank you for all of your help." This was another gratifying experience for me. For those who want to learn more about this condition, I recommend the book *Brain Allergies: The Psychonutrient Connection* by William Philpott, M.D., and Dwight Kalita, Ph.D.

Often, these diseases occur together and must be treated concurrently. For those who are interested in finding a physician familiar with the diagnosis and treatment of these illnesses, I recommend that you visit the following Web site: *http://www.ACAM.org*.

* * * * *

I continued to build my practice at Harmony Health Care, enjoying the autonomy and freedom of being able to run my own office. Some of my patients followed me from the other practice and others were referred by alternative healthcare providers in the area. Frequently, I would give lectures on such topics as alternative treatments for menopause, heart disease, and chronic fatigue syndrome. These lectures were well attended and generated a lot of interest in my practice.

On numerous occasions, I was a guest of Gary Null, a well-known nutritionist and pioneer in the field of alternative medicine, on his popular radio show that aired throughout the Tri-State area. After each interview ended, my phone would ring off the hook as people from New Jersey, Connecticut, and all five boroughs of New York called for appointments. I also appeared with Gary and other physicians on videos that aired on public television. He graciously referred to me as a "leading nutritionist" in his book, *Gary Null's Ultimate Lifetime Diet.*

During this time, I was also in charge of a physical rehabilitation program in Connecticut, working in conjunction with a group of chiropractors to whom I had been introduced while at my previous practice. Patients with chronic neck and lower back pain responded dramatically to this rehab program, which combined exercise, muscle strengthening, spinal adjustments, and physical therapy. Many of them were able to return to their normal activities and reduce or discontinue their pain medications. Even more important was that as a result of these treatments, the majority did not have to go under the surgeon's knife and deal with all the complications and pain associated with spinal surgery. I was impressed with these results and clearly saw the benefits of working as a team with chiropractors.

I had been working there for about a year when the lawyer who had drawn up the corporation papers for my rehabilitation center approached me with a business proposal. He said that he was retained by a group of chiropractors in New York who also wanted to form physical rehabilitation centers, (all of these would also be incorporated with the help of this attorney), where they would work in conjunction with physicians. His clients were looking for a medical doctor to own these rehab centers since in New York, only physicians could own medical corporations. Because of my experience with this business venture, he wanted to know if I was interested. As owner of my corporation in Connecticut, I was responsible for the oversight and supervision of the rehab program, but according to him, there would be a different set of responsibilities that I would have as an owner of a New York corporation.

He told me that I would still be sole shareholder of the corporation, just as I was in Connecticut, but my job duties would be limited to acting as a consultant to these corporations on an "as needed" basis. He said that it would not be necessary for me to be there on a regular basis, as I was at my Connecticut center, because there would be management companies running the day-to-day business operations of the centers and a staff of physicians would supervise the rehab program. In return for my services, I would be paid $333 per month. He also told me that according to the statutes in New York corporate law, there was no limit to the number of corporations that I could own.

I entered into this business venture because I believed in the concept of medical doctors working as a team with chiropractors in the treatment of musculoskeletal problems. In my personal experience, I had seen many patients who had participated in the physical rehab program have significant improvement in their symptoms. I also trusted this attorney because he was well respected in the area of healthcare law.

Over the next weeks to months, he sent me proposals from one chiropractor after another who was interested in having me own the various medical corporations. Eventually, I would own over thirty corporations, which for a while at least, gave me a comfortable financial cushion. Unfortunately my windfall would come to an abrupt end about eighteen months later when the FBI began to make the rounds at some of my corporations.

* * * * *

During this time, I was also still trying to find ways to expand my spiritual horizons. I began by reading *Autobiography by a Yogi* by Paramahansa Yogananda, who stressed the importance of meditation as a means to connect with God. Following his advice, I then started to meditate on a regular basis. Although this brought me a great deal of peace, I felt that I needed a way to put my spiritual knowledge into action. Although I was already doing this by striving to practice the Golden Rule, I felt that I needed to do more. But what?

My answer came when I was handed a book called *Random Acts of Kindness,* which took the adage that it is better to give than receive to a whole new level. The author of this book, who quite appropriately remains anonymous, claimed that doing good deeds anonymously would magnify the joy of giving tenfold. This sounded good to me so I decided to try it.

One day as I was traveling from Connecticut to New York to visit my parents, I stopped at the toll booth at the Throg's Neck Bridge and told the attendant that I was also paying for the car behind me. I was halfway across the bridge when a car came out of nowhere, the driver blasting his horn. The next thing I knew, he had pulled up beside me as though he was challenging me to a drag race, which was just a little more than insane considering our precarious location. I felt trapped with no place to exit and prepared to meet my Maker, only to turn and see that the driver was grinning from ear to ear and giving me the thumbs up sign. It was then that I realized that this was the gentleman whose toll I had just paid for a minute earlier. He was just trying to thank me. His gratitude brought a smile to my face. I recommend random acts of kindness as one of the best prescriptions for anyone who is suffering from depression. Not only will it lift the spirits of the giver, but it will also warm the heart of the receiver.

As it happened, that was the same day that I gave my father his first injection of testosterone. He had told me several months previously that his decreased libido was causing problems between him and Mom, who, he said, was "very vibrant." I told him that that was more than I needed to know and subsequently ordered a blood test to see if low levels of testosterone were the cause of his diminished sex drive. Indeed, his levels were well below normal and I recommended that he be started on bimonthly intramuscularly injections of testosterone.

Dad was only one of many men who, once they get past the age of fifty, have a significant decrease in the level of this hormone that not only results in a waning of libido, but can also contribute to the expanding waistlines, sagging muscles and crabby moods common to men in their midlife and beyond. High cholesterol and arteriosclerotic heart disease can also be exacerbated by deficiency of this important hormone. Physiologic replacement of testosterone often leads to the improvement of all these conditions.

Decreased libido in women who are postmenopausal can also be due to dropping levels of testosterone. The ovaries normally produce low levels of testosterone premenopausally, but during menopause these levels can drop precipitously, resulting in a decreased sex drive. Many women, as well as some doctors, think that this dwindling interest in sex is part of the "change of life," but I had often found that low levels of testosterone were commonly the cause of the problem and, by replacing this hormone, there was marked improvement in their libido.

In Dad's case, because the testosterone was in a viscous solution, I needed to inject it into a large muscle, preferably the *gluteus maximus*, or buttocks. Since he didn't want my mother to know that he was having this treatment, we needed to find a place which would give us some privacy, finally settling on their garage, which, though dark, dirty, and dusty, was the best clandestine place available to us. However, even here privacy was limited since, in this development, the garages were contiguous, separated only by metal fences that provided plenty of gaps for viewing.

"Can you imagine what our neighbor would think if he drove up and saw us in this position?" I said to my father as he stood bent over before me, his drawers dropped around his knees. That was over ten years ago and I still chuckle every time I think about it. The good news was that after a series of these injections, Dad told me that the shots were "working" and once again I told him that was all I needed to know. Fortunately, shortly after this, testosterone became available in cream form, which put an end to these top secret trips to the garage.

* * * * *

This interlude of tranquility in my life was soon to come to an end when chest X-rays done on my mother during a routine workup for a minor surgical procedure, revealed that she had lung cancer, the result of having been a heavy smoker for most of her life. The tumor was small and still in its early stages. This was fortunate, since in most patients, when lung cancer is first detected, it is in more advanced stages with a high probability of deadly metastasis and a survival rate of less than five years. Since a battery of tests did not show any evidence of metastasis, removal of the tumor would likely be curative. Furthermore, no chemo or radiation would be needed post-op. Another bit of good news was the fact that the tumor was in the upper lobe, which made it relatively accessible for surgical removal.

I was there for her surgery and when I went into see her, immediately post-op, I was shocked by what I saw. This powerhouse of a woman swaddled in blankets from the head down looked so incredibly vulnerable and fragile. My solar plexus tightened, literally taking my breath away, and my heart ached as I bent over and kissed her forehead. Fortunately, Mom fully recovered from the surgery and was as good as new, at least for a while.

The next challenge in my life, one that would last for the next four years, occurred in 1996. That year, I was reported to the Connecticut Department of Public Health regarding a patient that I had treated, a ten-year-old boy diagnosed with attention deficit hyperactivity disorder, commonly known as ADHD. He was brought to me by his mother because she did not want to start him on Ritalin® as their pediatrician had advised. She was concerned about the serious side effects associated with this medication and was hoping that I could offer treatment options that were safer and more effective than this drug. My battle with the department was triggered, in part, because of my "unconventional" approach to the treatment of this disorder.

Since this case played such a huge role in my life, I want to provide the reader with some background information concerning my treatment of ADHD. During my years in practice, I had found that the mood swings and problems with memory and concentration associated with ADHD could be caused or exacerbated by subclinical hypothyroidism and candidiaisis; two conditions that were mentioned previously.

After doing a thorough medical history, family history, and physical exam on this boy and taking into consideration his low basal body temperature, I concluded that he had hypothyroidism and started him on a low dose of Armour® thyroid. I did not get any thyroid blood tests because in his case I felt like I already had sufficient clinical information to make the diagnosis. The fact that I didn't get this blood test would come back to haunt me in the years that followed.

This child also had a history of being on repeated courses of antibiotics throughout his life for ear and upper respiratory infections. The history, coupled with the findings on physical exam, was consistent with a diagnosis of candidiaisis. After a month of treating him for both of these conditions, his memory and concentration started to improve and he was no longer hyperactive. As time went on, he continued to make progress and his mother was thrilled with the results. Everything was going well until suddenly I was caught in the crossfire of a battle between the boy's mother and her ex-husband.

She had full custody and had just asked him for an increase in child support. In an effort to avoid paying it, he was trying to prove that she was endangering his son's life. He began to attack every aspect of her life in order to prove his case, claiming that her conversion from being a Catholic to a Jehovah's Witness, which he considered to be a "fringe" religion, proved that she was unstable. When he found out that she had taken her son out of state and traveled to Connecticut to see a physician who practiced alternative medicine, which he considered quackery, I also became a target of his attack.

The problems started when he called my office, verbally abusing my staff and demanding a copy of his son's medical records. The boy's mother assured me that she had full say in her son's medical care, but I made her bring in the divorce agreement so that I could verify her claim. While reviewing this document, I came across a clause that clearly corroborated what she had told me. However, the father called my office relentlessly and continued to harass me. Finally, on one Sunday afternoon, when he called again demanding information, I relented, despite his abrasive manner, because as a father myself, I identified with his need to know what was going on with his child.

I was calm and patient as I explained the rationale behind my diagnosis and treatment plan. I also told him that I had used this treatment protocol for other children in my practice and, like his son, they had made significant improvement. Only when at the end of our conversation, he told me that it had been taped, did I realize his true intent. This man was trying to incriminate me, rather than being sincere in his desire to know the reasons for my treatment plan.

He then proceeded to report me to the Connecticut Department of Public Health. His new wife, a pediatric anesthesiologist, jumped on the bandwagon as well. She sent letters to physicians throughout the country, including the chairman of pediatrics at Johns Hopkins, a letter of which I was later able to obtain a copy, recommending that they write to the Connecticut Medical Board and demand that my license be revoked because of the "dangerous" protocol that I had used in treating children for ADHD.

About a month later, I received a letter from the Department of Public Health notifying me that it was launching an investigation into this case. A subsequent medical review concluded that I had not properly diagnosed and treated both hypothyroidism and candidiaisis and as a result, they recommended a number of sanctions be taken against me as well as fining me a hefty sum of money. I found it ironic that despite the fact that the child responded well to my treatment, with no side effects or any problems whatsoever, that I was being accused of rendering substandard care.

I met with a malpractice attorney, who after reviewing the case, concluded that I had done nothing wrong. He recommended that I challenge the Department of Public Health and take this case to trial before the medical board. Following his advice, I began a legal battle that would last close to four years, cost me thousands of dollars in legal fees, and added to the mounting emotional stresses that lay ahead, all of which would reach a critical mass and crush me in the process.

Another crisis then erupted later that year. I became involved in a major backlash from the insurance companies who were concerned when they started to receive bills that were three times higher than those they were accustomed to receiving from the corporations that I owned. They had requested the incorporation papers from each of my corporations and when my name appeared on over thirty documents as sole shareholder, it raised a big red flag.

Suspecting attempted fraud, the insurance companies notified the FBI, two representatives of which came knocking on the door of one of my corporations on Long Island. I had a good rapport with the chiropractor who worked there and, genuinely concerned about the implications that this had for me, he promptly called to tell me what was happening. The chiropractor had also trusted the advice of the "expert" healthcare attorney who had set up this corporation, but now he was suspicious of the information that he had been given.

Following his advice, I immediately contacted the new healthcare attorney that he had retained in order to get a second opinion about the legal quagmire that I was now facing. This attorney belonged to a prestigious law firm in Manhattan. Due to the urgency of the matter, he arranged a Saturday morning meeting at his office. As I walked into a conference room complete with a formidable mahogany table and soft leather chairs, I saw that he had also brought along another attorney. This gentleman was a former prosecutor who had experience with many cases involving healthcare fraud. He spent the next hour explaining all the pitfalls and legal problems that I could face if I continued ownership of these thirty-plus corporations. Among other startling revelations, he told me that, as owner of these corporations, I had many more responsibilities than I was originally told by the "expert" attorney whom I had first consulted.

As soon as he was finished, I wanted to know everything that I had to do in order to extricate myself from this legal fiasco. Fortunately, both attorneys were willing to help me. The ex-prosecutor advised that I immediately send out letters to the chiropractors involved, informing them that I was dissolving my corporations. And since this process would take about six months, he advised that, in the meantime, I become more active in these corporations during this time frame.

When I asked him what he meant by that, he told me that I needed to visit each office and audit the billing records and other financial statements of each corporation. It was also important to check the licensure status of each physician and healthcare professional at the various centers. Overwhelmed by all this information, I was glad to hear that I could also appoint representatives to assist me in this colossal endeavor since it was physically impossible for me to visit all thirty-seven corporations which were spread out all across New York City, Long Island, and upstate New York.

I appointed my mother and my good friend Vinny as representatives. I would soon find out that I was being betrayed by some of these chiropractors who were abusing the agreements that I in good trust had entered into with them. Later on I would pay the consequences for my naiveté.

The chiropractors were very upset, many threatening lawsuits after they received my letter. It was soon clear that it would a long time and thousands and thousands of dollars to untangle myself from this web of legal problems. But, a few years later, just when I thought that the storm had passed, this whole affair would resurface and explode into a major disaster that would have catastrophic professional, financial and emotional consequences for me.

In the background during this time, was my ongoing battle with the Department of Public Health, which was presenting their case against me to the medical board. The attorneys for the department called on expert witnesses who testified that my treatment of the ten-year-old boy with ADHD was not consistent with the generally accepted treatment of this condition, which was Ritalin. I was humiliated and ridiculed by the chairman of the medical board for my beliefs and principles in the practice of alternative medicine. With each attack, my confidence and self-esteem were chipped away. One of the physicians who was willing to testify in my defense did not cower in the face of the chairman's challenges during his testimony. Instead, he vigorously defended his position. After he finished his testimony, my lawyer whispered to me that I should follow his example and also be more aggressive in my defense, challenging the abuses of the draconian chairman at every opportunity. But by that time, my bravado and confidence had wilted and I was not up to the task.

While I made my way through this minefield of unending problems in my professional life, I tried to maintain a sense of normalcy in my personal life. In May of 1996, I met a woman on a blind date. As the evening progressed, I thought that this was also going to be our only date. The last thing on my mind was that she was going to be the next Mrs. Cohen.

Lisa was friendly, smiling and joking the entire evening, but there seemed to be no connection between us. I called her the next day and suggested that it might be better if we did not continue to see each other. She sounded disappointed, but said that she understood. I thought that this chapter was closed, until a few days later, when she sent me a sweet note that touched my heart. I was vulnerable at that time, being weighed down by all the stresses that I faced on a daily basis. As the weekend approached, feeling lonely and heavy-hearted, I called her for a date. Time would tell that I should have listened to my gut and not made that call.

After two weeks of dating, she urged me to move in with her, but I resisted. She was pleasant and fun to be with but I was not in love with her. Moving in was a commitment that I didn't want to make. However, with each passing day, she intertwined herself more and more into my life and because of my fragile emotional state, I enabled her in this process.

She had just lost her job and was worried about her finances. I needed to hire a new receptionist, so in order to help her, I offered her the job. As time went on, she repeatedly asked me to move in and I finally gave in to her request. We both benefited from the arrangement; she told me that she enjoyed doing my laundry, cooking my meals and running my errands, and at the time I was very much in need of a caretaker.

Even though I didn't feel the passion for her that I had for other women in my life, I began to think that I was being too unrealistic and idealistic in my concept of the perfect mate. I looked back and saw how my previous marriages had imploded despite the magic that was there at the onset and realized that I had been more in love with being in love and less eager to face reality. It seemed to me, at the time, that the main ingredient for a satisfying relationship was the ability to just get along, which we did. Passion was optional. So, after a year of living together, I decided to ask her to marry me. She was overjoyed.

We set the wedding date for early July 1997, but as the day approached, the gnawing in my gut telling me that this relationship, this marriage was wrong, finally reached a point where I could no longer ignore it. I decided to cancel the wedding, subsequently planning to cancel her job at the office as well. She was, understandably, upset over the change in our plans to be married, but was also still determined to continue our relationship and living arrangement. I wanted to move out and find someone else to work in my office, but as I became more and more overwhelmed by the other burdens that were building in my life, I did not have the will or emotional reserve to make these other changes. It was easier for me to maintain the *status quo* and that's exactly what I did.

As my legal problems intensified with the corporations and my trial with the medical board, I felt a certain restlessness stirring in my soul. An inner voice was telling me that I needed to change the way I practiced medicine and move on to my next level as a healer. But I didn't know what that would be. It was then that I heard about a conference on energy healing being given by an interesting woman, Barbara Brennan. This woman's background intrigued me.

She began her career as a physicist, working for NASA as a research scientist. As she delved deeper and deeper into the world of physics, she was led to the study of the "human energy field," the aura of energy that surrounds all of us and interpenetrates the physical body. Ms. Brennan, having succeeded in blending her knowledge of physics with the Eastern mystical teachings of chakras, had started a school to train people in the science of healing through working on the imbalances in the human energy field where disease first begins before eventually filtering into the body and producing illness.

When I discovered that she was offering a weekend

workshop in nearby New Jersey, Lisa and I enrolled, eager to incorporate this form of healing into my practice. We both found the conference inspiring. When I saw that she was as excited as me about the information that we had received, I began to think that we had more in common than I had first believed. As the next few months passed by, I decided that marriage might not be such a bad idea and finally, in September 1997, we married. After the wedding though, my gut was still telling me that I had made a mistake. Furthermore, as the next two years dragged by, I also found myself being pulled down deeper and deeper into the legal morass that was slowly suffocating me.

* * * * *

My plans to attend Barbara Brennan's school were put on hold when in May of 1999, my dad, who had a significant history of heart disease, was admitted to the hospital for a massive heart attack. In a coma and on life support, his cardiac function was minimal. However, his cardiologist, who dearly loved my father, did not want to give up on him and still maintained hope for his recovery.

My mother and my sister did not want to let him go and hovered around his bedside, holding his flaccid hand, begging him to fight back, to rally, and not to give up. After reviewing my father's medical chart, I knew that, if he survived, his quality of life would be dismal. As I stood by his bedside, tears streaming down my cheeks, I whispered, "Dad, its okay if you want to leave. You are going to a better place." Remarkably, he must have had some reason for not moving on because, even with his minimal cardiac function, Dad fought back and was soon well enough to be transferred out of the ICU onto a step-down unit on the medical floor. A miraculous recovery indeed, but after that, he was never the same.

During the time that he was in a coma, Dad's blood

supply to his brain had decreased, which led to decreased mental functioning and confusion with the result that after gaining consciousness, he was convinced that my mother had gone to California with his cardiologist for a romantic rendezvous. When I explained to my dad that, while he had been comatose, the disruption of oxygen to his brain might account for him hallucinating about my mother's affair, he looked at me in a way that made it clear that he comprehended my explanation but then said, in a strong voice, "Yeah, but I know that it happened!" While he was still recovering in his room in the ICU, he asked my mother to make him some scrambled eggs. When she told him that he was in the hospital and that there was no way that she could do this, he shouted, "I don't give a damn, just make me some eggs!"

My father's degree of cardiac output was so poor that fluid backed up into his lungs and he was in florid congestive heart failure. The simple act of breathing required tremendous effort, forcing his chest to heave with each gulp of air. When he was discharged from the hospital at the beginning of June, barely functional and bedridden, it was incredibly sad and painful to see him in such a debilitated state.

Then, on a Sunday afternoon in July as my mother was helping him back from the bathroom, he stumbled and crying out, "I can't take this anymore!" collapsed on the bed and died. I felt a sense of relief at his passing, knowing that his suffering was finally over. But my heart was gripped with pain when I realized that he would no longer be part of my life.

As I prepared my eulogy for Dad, I remembered so many things about him. How, when returning home after a long day's work, despite being tired and worn out, he always found the time to play baseball with me when I was in grade school. I also recalled that as a child, and even into my adult years, he always greeted me with a hug and a kiss. This became a little awkward during my adolescence when he displayed the same affection for me in front of my friends, but my love for my father far outweighed any sense of embarrassment and I welcomed his embrace.

My father was also my hero. On a hot summer day, when I was about eight years old, I was outside our apartment playing with a cat that I had just found when suddenly the cat's owner came out of nowhere and grabbed my arm. I cried out in pain as he tightened his grip and then, suddenly, Dad, with only a towel wrapped around his waist, barefoot, his face covered with shaving cream, came to my rescue! I will never forget that moment for as long as I live.

It didn't really hit me that my father was gone until I ran out of golf balls. My parents lived across the street from a golf course and there were plenty of duffers playing the links, so there was never a shortage of balls flying over the fence. Dad used to collect so many for me that I never had to buy them. One day while I was golfing, about two years after he passed away, I hit one of my many errant tee shots and lost my ball. I reached into my bag to replace it and was stunned to find that it was empty. It was only then that I fully realized that my father was no longer in my life.

* * * * *

The next crisis that I faced happened just two months after my father passed away. I was in my office, dealing with a difficult patient, when I took a quick bathroom break. As I was urinating, shock overcame me when I saw the toilet fill with blood. My medical instincts told me that this bleeding could have been due to bladder or kidney cancer, but since I had led a holistic lifestyle for close to twenty years, eating organic food, drinking purified water, taking supplements, exercising, and meditating, I "knew" that I was immune to cancer and was convinced that the most likely source for the bleeding was an infected prostate.

The following day I made an appointment with my urologist but while I was there, my urine sample was completely normal with no trace of blood. He did a urine culture looking for an infection, and gave me a prescription for antibiotics. I was scheduled for a CAT scan to rule out kidney or bladder cancer as the cause of my bleeding. I went home feeling confident that prostatitis was the correct diagnosis. But my confidence would be shot down that night when, during another routine trip to the bathroom, I noticed large clots of blood in my urine. Soon the stream was blocked, putting me into acute urinary retention that necessitated the insertion of a catheter to empty my bursting bladder as soon as I arrived in the emergency room.

I was admitted to the hospital and the CAT scan, which was to have been done on an outpatient basis, was now an emergency procedure. As I waited for what appeared to be an interminable period of time for my urologist to call me with the results, my anxiety became overwhelming. I called his office, beseeching him for the results of the tests. His hesitation made it obvious that he wanted to deliver the news in person, but I persisted and was floored when he told me that I had a cancerous tumor, the size of an orange, clinging to the upper pole of my right kidney.

My first response was to ask him if he was certain, not meaning to insult his medical acumen, but because I was still encased in a thick armor of shock and denial. But in the end, there was no way to escape the truth. I was forced to face the diagnosis that we all fear the most. I had cancer.

Chapter Six

After I had finally accepted the fact that I did have cancer, the next step was to do diagnostic tests to make sure that it had not metastasized. If that was the case, my prognosis would have been very poor. Still, despite this distinct possibility, somehow I knew in my heart that the cancer had not spread. All the tests, including a bone scan, confirmed what my inner voice was telling me. They all turned out to be negative. I was discharged from the hospital that Friday, scheduled for surgery to remove my kidney the following Monday.

This was the longest weekend of my life. Thoughts of all shapes and sizes zigzagged through my mind. My feelings filled the spectrum from fear to anger to despair and deep grief. Finally, I focused on gratitude. I was grateful that, although it is common for kidney cancer to metastasize, mine had not. Because the kidney is tucked away in the part of the body known as the retroperitoneum where there are no other vital organs to impede its growth, the cancer is free to increase in size with minimal to no symptoms. This means that in most cases by the time it is diagnosed, the cancer has long since spread to vital structures and organs. The same is true for pancreatic and ovarian cancer. But thankfully, my body had signaled the presence of this tumor by producing blood in the urine, leading to the diagnosis of this aggressive cancer before it had a chance to spread.

There was also another blessing. This cancer that I was carrying, although greatly serious in its potential consequences, had occurred in an organ in which I had a spare. I remembered the words of the nephrologist under whom I had studied while in medical school. He had compared the risk of having only one kidney to the risk of always driving five miles above the speed limit: The potential for danger was always lurking but could be avoided by exerting extra caution and living a healthy lifestyle.

On the Sunday night before the operation, both my dear friend Anthony and my mother came up from New York to sleep over so that they could be there in the morning for my surgery. Since I had left the church years back, my mother's attitude towards me had softened and I welcomed her love and support. I was also deeply touched and surprised that Anthony was willing to make the three-hour trip from eastern Long Island to Connecticut and spend hours in the waiting room just to make sure that he would be there for me when I awakened from the surgery. We had been friends for a long time. I had attended his wedding, watched his two kids grow up, and was his family physician, but this seemed to be above and beyond the call of duty. When I asked him why he was making this sacrifice, he told me that he loved me. His devotion was a great source of comfort. Anthony would be a bastion of strength for me in the dark days that lay ahead.

We arose early Monday morning and my wife drove me and my entourage to the hospital. After the admitting procedure and pre-op orders were completed, I was directed to my room, waiting for the moment when they would take me on the journey to the OR. When that time finally came, I remember getting on the stretcher and feeling like I was going to my execution as they rolled me towards the elevator that led to the operating room. As a physician, I knew all the potential complications that could occur during surgery and, as a consequence, it was a particularly disturbing experience to be on the receiving end of the knife.

The next thing I remember was waking up in the recovery room to find Anthony and my family gathered around me, anxious and helpless to relieve my pain. As it turned out, the anesthesiologist who was supposed to be there to manage my post-op pain was stuck in labor and delivery and couldn't get to me in time. Finally, he rushed to my side, started an intravenous morphine drip that allowed me to drift off into a blissful sleep. The surgery had gone well and the urologist had more good news for me: the tumor was well encapsulated, which further reduced the chance of there being any metastasis. I was extremely relieved because the pathology report revealed a high-grade aggressive form of kidney cancer and if it had spread, my prognosis would have been abysmal.

Meanwhile, I spent four miserable days in the hospital, stapled together like a cardboard box. Weak and debilitated, every move produced a lancing pain in my side. Just getting out of bed to use the bathroom was a major accomplishment. Food, usually a source of great enjoyment for me, had no appeal. It was humbling to lie helplessly in bed, following the doctor's orders, when I was always the one giving the orders.

Following discharge, I went home and took only a week off because I was eager to get back to my practice. In retrospect, I should have taken more time off. My body was still recovering from the trauma of the surgery as it made the physiological adjustments necessary to working with only one kidney. Furthermore, I was still scarred from the recent passing of my father, a wound that my face-to-face confrontation with cancer had only deepened.

I was still searching for answers as to why I had developed this dreaded disease. Was it hereditary? There was a strong family history of cancer in my family: with my father, it had involved his colon; my sister, the breast; and my mother, the lung. But, in fact, none of these cancers increased my risk of developing kidney cancer. I knew that it wasn't my lifestyle habits, because for twenty years I had followed all of the recommendations given to reduce the risk of getting cancer. I needed to dig deeper.

In my studies, I had learned that most disease started from emotional, mental, or spiritual imbalances, so my search for an answer was aimed in that direction. My therapist poignantly revealed to me that not only do the kidneys filter out poisons and toxins from the physical body, but on another level, they filter emotions as well. Along this line of reasoning, she added that if emotional toxins such as hatred, anger, and resentment overload the kidney, then, over time, it was quite possible that they could coalesce into a cancerous tumor. This made sense to me because of my lifetime battle against self-hatred. Later on, in my study of acupuncture, I would also learn that the kidneys were particularly vulnerable to the destructive effects of fear. This emotion was another nemesis in my lifelong fight with depression.

Interestingly, I also learned in my studies of traditional Chinese medicine that grief is stored in the lungs. This helped me realize that my childhood history of chronic asthma could have been related to the grief I carried from not receiving the unconditional love from my mother; the sort of love that I so desperately needed while I was growing up. Also, Mom's grief over the loss of her mother could have been another factor that contributed to the etiology of her lung cancer.

In addition, studies have revealed that holding onto feelings of anger – not high cholesterol, high blood pressure, or even smoking – is the number one risk factor for developing heart disease. More recently it has been shown that one can actually die from a "broken heart." Emotional trauma is what triggers the broken-heart syndrome and it can unleash a cascade of physiological changes that directly stress the heart and produce symptoms similar to those experienced during an actual heart attack. Research has also shown that those women who have felt emotionally stunted or suppressed by their husbands or significant other were at a much higher risk of developing breast cancer than their counterparts who were in healthy relationships.

This knowledge, though important, did not stop me from sliding into a deep depression as fall turned into winter and the cumulative effect of many factors in my life were reaching a frenzied crescendo. The ongoing stress and strain from my battle with the medical board, the entangled legal dilemma with the corporations, the legal fees that were siphoning my financial reserves, the debilitating physical and emotional effects from my surgery, the deep grief that I still had from the loss of my father, and being in a marriage that was not bringing me any joy all combined to drain my emotional reserves. I felt as though despair and darkness were sucking the breath of Life from my soul.

My thoughts turned to suicide as the only way to escape this endless misery. Many see taking one's life as the ultimate act of cowardice, weakness, and selfishness. But I can tell you from my personal experience that the emotional pain that drives one to this final act of desperation is so intense, so unrelenting, so merciless and unforgiving, that death seems like the only option left to end the intolerable suffering. One Saturday morning in late January 2000, I made the preparations that would ensure my final exit from this life.

That day, Lisa would be away visiting her sister. She seemed concerned about my emotional disquietude and was worried about leaving me alone, but I had taken pains to hide the true depths of my anguish. After she left, I grabbed the two bottles of medication that would lead me painlessly out of this life. One contained eighty pills of the sedative Ativan®, the other, fifty pills of the sleeping medication Ambien®. I was in a quandary as to where to take this deadly combination of medication. Wanting to spare my wife the shock of finding me dead at home, I got into my car and began to search for a secluded location where I would not be found until after the medications reached the critical blood levels necessary to transport me to my ultimate destination.

I merged onto the highway with the two bottles within easy reach on the passenger seat. Each time I passed an exit, my eyes searched for a location that would serve my purposes. As each exit whizzed by, not even hinting of a place that would ensure my privacy, any remnants of sanity that I still possessed evaporated, and I swallowed the contents of both bottles while driving in the thick of traffic. The last thing I remember before losing consciousness was exiting the highway. My next memory was waking up in the emergency room of a nearby hospital, my mind shrouded in a drug-induced haze. I was later told that soon after I left the highway there were no other cars around as I crashed head on into a lamppost and totaled my car. Somehow, I was left unscathed.

* * * * *

After recovering from the overdose, I was transferred to a locked unit at Silver Hill Psychiatric Hospital in New Canaan, Connecticut. This hospital has an excellent reputation and many famous people from the entertainment industry have entered the doors of this facility for treatment. Silver Hill was set in a secluded location, surrounded by rolling hills and meadows, an environment that was very conducive to healing. Ultimately, my accommodations were luxurious for a hospital; each patient had a tastefully furnished private room and bath, and meals were served in a quaint cafeteria. With all that this facility had to offer, one patient joked that the name of the hospital should have been changed to *The Silver Hilton.*

However, this wing of the hospital was located in an area outside of the locked unit and it would be necessary for me to first dig myself out of my deep depression before I could graduate to that level of care. The initial unit to which I was confined was a single floor which surrounded a nurses' station that was encased in towering walls of Plexiglas. Each room, though clean and neat, had only the basic necessities and none of the luxuries associated with the rest of the hospital.

During each depressive episode it seemed as if my dark side emerged from the shadows and took full possession of my soul. Upon admission, I was disheveled, barely communicative, disconnected, and disassociated from reality. I was filled with so much fear and anxiety that it was a tremendous effort for me to even speak. Soon after the intake was done by the nurse, I was strip-searched by an aide to make sure that I was not sneaking in any contraband. This was a humiliating experience. Even though I knew that it was done for my own good, I still felt debased, violated, and stripped of any trace of dignity.

As the next few days passed, I wandered the hallways, my mind short-circuited by an overload of thoughts and worries that streamed across the billions of synapses in my brain. Now I would have to face all the problems that I was trying so desperately to escape. What was going to happen to my medical practice? Who would take care of my patients? What was going to happen to my medical license? Where was I going to get the money to pay for the mounting legal bills that I was facing? All of these thoughts took turns dancing in my brain repeating the same steps over and over again.

But the solutions came. My staff was able to find another physician to cover my practice. Anthony would once again come to my rescue and lend me money to cover my legal expenses. But even with these fears assuaged, I still felt hollow, empty, hopeless. My wife tried to raise my spirits by bringing in a card that glowed with praise for my help from a patient that I had treated recently. Instead of giving me solace, this card only brought me even more grief because I felt like the doctor that she was referring to had vacated my soul forever and in its place was a weak, useless, shell of a man.

My friend Vinny also reached out to help me. One visiting day, he brought his dad whom I had treated for heart disease, using diet, nutritional supplements, and intravenous treatments. His father gave me a pep talk, reminding me of how much I had helped him as well as other patients. However, because of my distorted view of reality, I felt like he was mocking me and I fell into even deeper depths of despair.

I was not responding to the antidepressant medication and as I continued to waste away, becoming more and more withdrawn, my psychiatrist, an expert in the field of ECT, decided that this treatment was the best course of therapy for me. He talked this over with my wife and mother and both agreed to this treatment, as did I. It was after the third treatment that a spark of hope, a sense of joy was rekindled in my heart.

I actually looked forward to my ECT treatments because, as the short-acting barbiturate began flowing through my bloodstream, slowly putting me into a state of unconsciousness in preparation for the procedure, my paralyzing anxiety melted away, leaving me in a state of peace that was incredibly healing. After each treatment was over, I awoke on my stretcher, snuggled in soft, warm cotton blankets, feeling blissful as the remnants of this medication continued to erase any memory of my gut wrenching fear and angst.

I don't know if it was the slow but steady dissolution of my anxiety caused by these medications, or the change in brain chemistry thought to occur from the induction of a seizure, or a combination of both, but after receiving a series of these treatments, the cloak of death that was smothering my soul lifted. As it did, my mood steadily improved. I was now able to take the first steps on my journey back to wellness.

ECT literally saved my life. I was fortunate to have only minor short-term memory loss, which, as I mentioned previously, is the most common side effect associated with this procedure. However, it does have other risks and side effects, some relatively minor such as headaches, malaise, and muscle aches and others potentially more serious. There is also no guarantee that everybody will have the same brisk response that I did. Nonetheless, I still think that it can be a valuable tool in the treatment of intractable depression.

As my condition continued to improve, I was transferred to the other wing of the hospital where the freedom to go outside and roam the beautiful grounds also contributed to my recovery. However, I was still in denial, determined to think of these episodes as examples, not of depression, but as flukes, aberrations, not part of who I truly was. These ECT treatments, although incredibly helpful, would only be Band-Aids that temporarily covered up the wound in my psyche that made me prone to the darkness of depression. It would not be until I faced my problems head on that I would be free of its grip. Unfortunately, nothing had been done to permanently put an end to the depressive episodes that would continue to increase in severity and frequency as time went on. I would leave the hospital after a two-week stay, the conquering hero, thinking that I was invincible, not knowing that I would be back there again before the year ended.

I was discharged on Valentine's Day 2000, which, ironically enough, did not turn out to be as good an omen for my marriage as one might expect. Upon returning home, I was buoyed by an exhilarating rush of energy, thanks again to my hypomania, which gave me a newfound strength and confidence. I no longer felt burdened by all the difficulties that had led me down the road of self-destruction. I was ready to face these problems and among them was my marriage, a marriage that was suffocating me. Now that I had the courage to take steps to improve this situation, I decided that a contributing factor as to why I was feeling so burdened by this relationship was due in part because my wife worked in my office. This situation only increased the tension between us and gave me little breathing room. I needed space.

I suggested to Lisa that our marriage might be strengthened if she found another job, taking pains to assure her that I would gladly support her until she found a job that she really liked. Her response was not at all what I expected. Exploding into a fit of rage, she told me that if she couldn't work in my office, I could no longer live in her house. Her tirade shocked me. She had always been so loving and thoughtful. I was trying to save our marriage but she saw things differently.

In retrospect, I can understand how she seamlessly interwove our working relationship and our marriage. She feared that once she left my office, it would only be a matter of time before our marriage ended. Unfortunately, by allowing her anger and bitterness to consume her, she created the very situation that she was trying to avoid, which set the stage for the dissolution of our marriage. I moved out and within a matter of months we were divorced.

Although it was difficult for her, I knew that it was absolutely the right thing for me to do. Fortunately as time passed, she found the strength to forgive me. Lisa eventually became involved in another relationship that brought her a lot of pleasure. She had stood by me during my darkest hours and her happiness helped free me from the guilt that I felt about the breakup of our marriage. I celebrated her joy.

My own happiness though, was short-lived. Just as I was feeling better and ready to take on the world, another crisis erupted. In March of 2000, the four major insurance companies that had been investigating my corporations for insurance fraud filed a $60 million racketeering lawsuit against me and all the chiropractors and physicians who had anything to do with the many corporations that I had previously owned. I was shocked to learn that while I was receiving $333 per month from each corporation, these facilities billed out over $20 million to the insurance companies. Most of these corporations were not taking advantage of the system, but those that were did so on a huge scale. Even though I had terminated my agreements with these corporations several years earlier, this lawsuit covered the time frame when I was still their owner, which sucked me into this legal disaster.

The punches came fast and furious, knocking me down, but not out, not yet. Soon after that, an article appeared in *The New York Times* calling me a "one-man walking fraud unit." I was then further rattled when the FBI came to my office, telling me that I was going to have to appear in front of a grand jury. Later on, my lawyer called my office to warn me that a reporter from *The New York Post* was coming up to Connecticut in order to interview me. My attorney advised that I not speak to him and have my receptionist say that I had no comment.

In July, a reporter and photographer finally made

their appearance at my office and I dutifully followed orders. "No comment" were the only words they heard from my receptionist. That was that, or so I thought. As the day ended, I changed into my shorts and sneakers, and got ready to go the gym. I tossed my brief case, a thermal insulated lunch bag, and a gym bag over my shoulder and as I was getting into my car, a voice called out to me, "Dr. Cohen!" I whirled around to see who was calling my name. Crouching on the ground before me was the photographer from the *Post* who had waited eight hours just for the opportunity to take my picture. I had my own paparazzi! Looking at her with a mixed expression of disdain and surprise, she snapped my picture, which ended up being splashed across the front page of the Sunday edition of *The New York Post*. Next to my photo were the words, emblazoned in large bold print: *RENT-A-DOC.*

Inside the newspaper there was a story in which I and the other physicians named in the suit were portrayed as modern-day versions of Jesse James and his gang of outlaws who were robbing insurance companies blind. This was my fifteen minutes of fame that came about in a most unfortunate way. And although I was mortified about this sort of publicity, I was relieved when my lawyer assured me that this story would soon be yesterday's news and that no one would remember it. But much to my chagrin, the first patient who came into my office the following Monday morning said to me, "Dr. Cohen, I read about you in the paper. What's going on?" I assured him that it was nothing to worry about and he didn't question me further.

My mother tried to comfort me as only my mother could. After seeing the full-length photo in the paper of me in my shorts she said, "Well, your legs look nice." I have kept a copy of that paper as a souvenir, a reminder of one of the many unexpected twists and turns my life has taken and how I summoned the strength and fortitude to surmount each challenge.

I did have a respite from bad news when that same month, my case with the medical board was finally resolved after four long years. When all the facts were in, the board fined me a thousand dollars and mandated that I get thyroid blood tests for all patients that I was working up for thyroid disease in the future. I have always tried to learn from the painful lessons that I experienced in life and this was no exception. This time, I learned to keep more complete medical records.

Previous to this case, my notes were scanty and, like most doctors, fairly illegible. Some physicians think that if their notes can't be read, that this shields them from any potential medical investigation or liability. The opposite is true. Most investigators assume the worst when they can't read the medical records and this only increases the physician's liability. More importantly, it is in the patient's best interest that the notes be legible. This minimizes mistakes and allows other doctors and healthcare providers who care for the patient to have a clear and concise idea of the diagnosis and medical treatment that had been rendered previously. With this in mind, I started to write legible notes that included in great detail every aspect of the patient's medical history and treatment plan.

In the meantime, the mounting pressures from the gargantuan lawsuit involving my corporations gradually began to take its toll on my sanity. My bouts of depression never struck me suddenly, with full force, but rather they began insidiously, with the damage beyond my conscious awareness. Only when the weight of despair became too heavy to carry did my psyche crumble. And by this time it was often too late to rectify the damage.

That is what happened to me when autumn dissolved into winter. The arrival of winter was a motif that frequently played in the background, as I slipped into the empty blackness of depression. It wouldn't be until a few years later that I would find out that it was common for the symptoms of bipolar disorder to be triggered or exacerbated during this season. As each day passed and the deadness of winter began to surround me, it became more and more difficult for me to get out of bed and charge into the world. Instead, all I wanted to do was to hide under the covers, hoping that Life would just go away and leave me alone.

Then, in December 2000, the anchor of depression that was trying to take me down into the dark seas of black despair finally became so heavy that I could no longer resist its pull. One morning, I took six tranquilizers, not a high enough dose to end my life, but enough to land me first in the emergency room and then back to Silver Hill Hospital.

Chapter Seven

On December 11, 2000, I once again entered the locked unit at Silver Hill Hospital. Suicidal thoughts were not plaguing me, but I was despondent, hopeless, numb, unable to concentrate, my mind in the grips of a disabling mental paralysis. Based on my previous brisk response to ECT, my psychiatrist recommended another series of these treatments.

Willing to surrender all the power and control that came with the role of being a physician and do everything that my psychiatrist recommended, I offered no resistance. My priority was to be restored to a level of wellness that would allow me to return to the profession that I loved so much.

Reversing roles and becoming a patient in my battles with both depression and cancer offered a blessing in disguise. The pain and suffering that I endured had increased my empathy and compassion for my patients and indeed, all people who suffer and are weighed down by the challenges of life.

With the completion of four inpatient ECT treatments, my mood improved dramatically and I was well enough to be discharged after an eleven-day hospital stay. I continued these treatments on an outpatient basis, and by the beginning of the New Year, was able to return to my practice. I was euphoric as I stepped into my office after being away for over three weeks. As I finally emerged from the depths of my depression, my appreciation for every aspect of life was intensified a thousandfold.

All was well until the summer of 2001 when in July,

my world was rocked again by the news that my mother, who had been on a perpetual diet for as long as I could remember in an effort to lose a few pounds, told me her appetite had decreased and she was shedding weight without dieting. She was also feeling tired. Mild weight loss, decreased appetite, and fatigue are all symptoms common to depression and, clearly, Mom was still mourning the loss of my father. However, my medical instincts told me to dig deeper, since she had been diagnosed a few years back with lung cancer. It was true that her cancer had been caught in its early stages; nonetheless, I knew that these symptoms, although subtle and nonspecific, could also have been due to a recurrence of that disease.

I immediately called her physician and shared my concerns with him, strongly suggesting that he do a complete medical workup. He sounded a little perturbed, probably thinking that I was overreacting and that my medical judgment was being clouded by my emotions. Reluctantly, he agreed to do the workup. One week later, he called me back, sheepishly admitting that my clinical instincts had been correct. Mom's lung cancer had metastasized to her liver and now this vital organ was infiltrated by this deadly disease. Needless to say, the prognosis for her survival was bleak. My worst fears now surfaced. I realized that I was going to lose my mother.

I refused to accept this. There was no way I was going to let her go, at least not without a fight. Like many physicians in the field of integrative medicine, I had often treated cancer patients with nutritional intravenous treatments as an adjunct to the radiation or chemotherapy that they were receiving. The IVs contained high doses of vitamin C and other vital nutrients and gave impressive results. Those patients who received these IVs not only had greater benefits from the chemotherapy and radiation, but also had a significant reduction in side effects from these treatments.

I also recommended to these patients a regimen of oral supplements as well as dietary changes, both of which have a major impact in boosting the immune system's ability to fight cancer. The use of nutritional supplements both oral and intravenous as a powerful tool in the armamentarium in the fight against cancer is well documented in such books as *Immunopower* by Patrick Quillin, Ph.D., and *Vitamin C, Infectious Diseases, and Toxins, Curing the Incurable*, by Thomas E. Levy, M.D., J.D. I was determined to use this nutritional approach to help my mom in her battle with cancer. She agreed, with one stipulation: she also wanted to get the opinion of an oncologist.

I was not much in favor of treating my mother's cancer with chemotherapy or radiation. Overall, the quality of her life was still good. She was not in pain and was still able to work and enjoy all of her favorite activities. Besides, I was concerned that, not only would the side effects from chemo or radiation significantly reduced her ability to enjoy life but they also would not offer much benefit at this late stage of her illness. Even after I voiced my concerns, she was still determined to see the oncologist. After a while, I gave up on my efforts to dissuade her. I did insist, however, on going with her for the consultation. Mom smiled. I could tell that she greatly appreciated my concern and involvement in her treatment.

After reviewing my mother's medical records, the oncologist recommended that she be started on what he referred to as "light chemo," which, he said, would have only minimal side effects. Since my mother wanted to have these treatments, I reluctantly agreed with one proviso: she would come up to my office on a weekly basis for nutritional IVs. I also prescribed a regimen of nutritional supplements. To my relief, she was more than happy to comply and dutifully followed my "orders."

The anger, the pain, the resentment that had frozen my heart and prevented me from loving her freely quickly melted away when I realized that I might lose her forever. I began to view her in a new light. Beyond the wall she had erected to defend herself from pain, beyond the anger, I saw the young girl who was still suffering the wounds resulting from the tragic loss of her mother and, filled with compassion, I forgave her for all the suffering that she had caused me.

This shift in my perception drew my mother closer to me. I embraced her with love and tenderness, trying to spend as much time with her as possible and calling her daily to "check in." Every Sunday, we would go see what she called an "artsy-fartsy" movie. Afterward, over dinner, we would engage in heated discussions about the merits of the film. I was thrilled when I overheard my mother tell a neighbor that I was her best friend.

In my eyes, this strong, independent woman was now as fragile as a china doll, although, in truth, she was still quite capable of taking care of herself. The cancer, although lodged in her liver, was not causing any serious symptoms and she still maintained her zest for life. Still, I became very protective, watching over her like a mother hen.

Since the ninety-minute drive from her home in Queens to my office in Connecticut was more than I thought that she could handle, I insisted on sleeping over and driving her back and forth. Mom thought that I was overreacting. In retrospect, I was. So, we reached a compromise. She would take a bus from Queens into Manhattan and then transfer to a train that would transport her to a station close to my office where one of my staff could pick her up. Although this was more cumbersome and time consuming than driving straight to my office, she was willing to make the sacrifice in order to please me.

My mother took this mode of transportation for a couple of weeks until she had enough of this marathon expedition and then, as always, decided to take matters into her own hands. One day, I had just completed a consultation and found to my surprise that she had arrived for her IV an hour early, having driven herself to my office rather than take the train. I suppose I should have been angry with her, but, instead, I had to laugh. "That's Mom," I thought. The iron woman would never go down without a fight. Actually, I was quite happy to see that she still had the strength and stamina to take care of herself. My mother had an excellent response to these IVs as her energy and appetite continued to improve. Fortunately, as well, the "light chemo" was not causing her any side effects.

Everything was going smoothly in my world until February 2002 when I started a relationship with a woman that would trigger my next episode of severe depression before the summer of '02 was over. I found her to be engaging, kind, and intelligent. Like me, she was also on a spiritual path. Her educational credentials impressed me as well. They included a B.A. with honors from Harvard University, an M.A. from the School of Arts and Sciences at the University of Pennsylvania, as well as an M.B.A. from the Wharton School. But what impressed me most was her willingness to give up what promised to be a lucrative career in the business world and pursue her passion of becoming a body-centered psychotherapist, specializing in spiritual transformation and tantra, a Sanskrit term for sacred sex. She had also traveled to Hawaii to study the ancient art of Kahuna healing in order to incorporate that modality into her practice as well.

This woman fascinated me. I was strongly attracted to her keen mind and interest in mastering the ancient healing arts. She also felt a strong attraction to me and within a week of meeting each other, we fell in love. Someone once said, "Those who fail to learn from history are doomed to repeat it." I was no exception. I repeatedly rushed into relationships with disastrous results, but I had not learned from these experiences. This time, the lesson would have horrendous consequences for me.

I had gladly surrendered my heart, soul, and mind to this woman. As a result of diving into this relationship, neither of us ever had the chance to get to know each other. When she eventually rejected me, the trauma would be irreparable. In the first few months, there were rumblings of her dissatisfaction with me. With the passage of time, as our imperfections rose to the surface, the friction between us grew until it reached a breaking point. Her final rebuff in late

July ripped me apart. Soon, my entire being was held captive by overwhelming anxiety and panic.

As August began, sleep escaped me for days at a time, setting the stage for what was now a familiar descent into a world of chaos and confusion. My judgment was impaired and my view of reality became distorted as the lack of sleep took its toll on my sanity. I couldn't go back to my practice. Fortunately, my staff immediately found a doctor to cover for me and, by the end of August, I was back at my mom's apartment in Queens, waiting for the storm that I was trapped in to pass. But Mom had other plans for me.

Perhaps it was because her patience was worn thin from having to deal with all of my previous episodes of depression. Her nerves may also have been frayed by the insidious effects that the cancer was slowly but surely having on her health. Whatever the reason, her ultimatum filled me with terror: if I didn't go back to work, she would have me admitted to the psychiatric hospital. The thought of being institutionalized again was too much for me to bear, so I weakly acquiesced to her demands and together, we made the long journey back to my office.

When we arrived, the office was empty except for my nurse who was finishing her work for the day, all the patients having already been seen by the doctor who was covering my practice. Leaving my mother in the outer office, I went into my consultation room and sank into my chair, completely unraveled by lack of sleep. I looked at all the diplomas and awards that decorated the walls and a sense of incredible grief overcame me as I mourned the loss of my sanity. My inability to maintain the role of physician, a profession to which I had dedicated my life, a profession that I cherished, was so crushing that it drove me to an act of desperation.

Calling the pharmacy, I ordered a prescription for thirty Ativan®. Then slipping out of the office, I walked to the pharmacy, which was only a short distance away, and picked up this medication. After sneaking back into my office, I quickly swallowed all of the pills. I didn't want to die. I didn't want to be hospitalized again either. I only wanted to escape the pain that was searing my soul. As this medication flowed through my bloodstream, I slowly drifted off into the sweet ecstasy of sleep.

* * * * *

I found out later that when I did not respond to my nurse's attempts to call me on the telephone intercom, both she and my mother rushed into my consultation room not knowing what to expect. After finding me lying unconscious on the floor, an empty bottle of pills next to me, they quickly surmised what I had done. This dose of the medication was not high enough to be fatal, but it induced a long, deep sleep from which I eventually awoke.

As I slowly floated back to reality, I noticed my mother standing next to my stretcher, clearly distraught. She was, I later learned, aware that I would make a complete recovery from this overdose. She also knew that once again I was going to be hospitalized. In her eyes I saw the glint of fear, fear that once she was gone, there would be nobody left to care for me. Worse yet, she feared that eventually I would lose my battle against depression and finally succeed in taking my own life. I squeezed her hand, trying to reassure her that everything was going to be okay, but I could tell that this did not alleviate her worries.

With my condition stabilized, it was time to transport me to my next destination, which I assumed was going to be Silver Hill. Memories of this hospital, that had been so conducive to my healing in the past, filled me with hope. This time, however, because of changes in my health insurance, I was denied the luxury of living among the rolling hills in New Canaan and instead was transported to the confines of a stark, desolate state hospital. I arrived there in a disoriented, disheveled state, fighting off the remnants of the Ativan® that was still circulating in my bloodstream.

During my admission process, I demanded to have the ECT treatments that had been so helpful to me in the past. But I was told that this therapy was not available at that institution. After hearing that, any hopes of a quick recovery faded from my mind.

I was shown to my room, which I shared with two other patients, no private rooms being available on the floor. I was once again on a locked unit with no escape, nowhere to go. I met dead ends everywhere I paced, except for the three times a day when we were allowed to go outside for twenty-minute increments. I was prescribed a new antidepressant and a low dose of an antipsychotic medicine, taken at bedtime to help me sleep. This medication, however, only added to my confusion and disorientation just as the bleakness of this place only deepened my despair and hopelessness. My mother, although worn out by my many encounters with depression, did not desert me. She drove over two hours from her apartment in Queens in order to visit me as often as she could.

After being there for a week, August gave way to September and my forty-ninth birthday rolled around. Instead of being a day of celebration, it turned into a day of mourning as I languished in the confines of this dismal psychiatric unit. When I was told that my attending psychiatrist had reported me to the Connecticut Department of Public Health because I had self-prescribed Ativan®, despair overwhelmed me. My mounting episodes of depression also had to be brought to the department's attention. I understood that the intention was to protect myself and the public, but I feared that I would lose my medical license forever and this fear fed the anxiety that was paralyzing my mind.

I now felt like I had nothing to live for. My self-identity was linked to my role as a physician. This profession defined who I was. If I were to lose my license to practice, my sense of purpose, my sense of self would dissolve. These thoughts crippled any resolve that I could muster which would help me crawl out of this dark canyon of helplessness and despondency

Incapacitated by grief, I found myself unable to participate in any of the group therapy programs. At the end of one of these sessions, the therapist, who assumed that I was not making any effort to get well, added insult to injury by saying, "Alan, if you don't make an effort to get well, you have three options: repeated hospitalizations, prison or death." This was tough love taken to an extreme.

When I was paid a visit by the head of the Impaired Physicians Program, a glimmer of hope shone through the dark cloud that followed me everywhere I went. This was a program established by the Connecticut Medical Society designed to help physicians who suffered from psychiatric disorders and substance abuse. I discovered that, under the program's auspices after discharge, I would be able to retain my license and return to practice if I met certain requirements.

First, I would have to be evaluated by a psychiatrist, of the program's choosing, who would determine if I was of sound mind and capable of returning to practice. In addition, I would have to find an approved doctor who would be willing to come to my office on a daily basis to make sure that I was practicing with "skill and safety." Finally, I would have to submit to random biweekly urine drug testing. The idea of ever being well enough to be discharged, let alone fulfill these requirements, was so beyond my grasp at that time that this information only deepened my anguish.

One day melted into the next. Eventually I became so overwhelmed by depression that I started to think of ways to escape the misery of being in this locked unit. I decided to starve myself, thinking that if I did, they would have to transfer me to the hospital for intravenous feedings. Even though the hospital was far from being a vacation spot, in my mind, anything was better than staying where I was. As a result, I fasted for about a week but eventually hunger won out and I started to eat.

After this plan failed, I determined to create a medical emergency that would transport me off the unit and into the hospital. Sticking pens deeply into my rib cage, I tried to pierce the thick musculature that protected the lungs and induce a collapsed lung. This act of lunacy only caused deep imprints of pen marks in my chest wall but before the year ended, my insane plan would succeed.

I concealed my attempts of self-destruction from everyone on the floor, including my psychiatrist. September finally yielded to October and after five weeks of being hospitalized, I was considered to be fit enough for discharge. This assessment was far from accurate. As I crossed the threshold of the hospital grounds to return home, things would only go from bad to worse.

After discharge, I continued to float in a sea of confusion. I lived in purgatory, my life on hold, caught in limbo, not yet well enough to return to practice, but so overcome by anxiety that I was incapable of making even the first steps towards wellness. I did not know what to do with all the free time and freedom that was suddenly thrust upon me. In mid-November, my psychiatrist gave me a prescription for Buspar®, a non-narcotic medication, used for the treatment of anxiety. When I left his office and started to drive home along a parkway lined with trees stripped of all their leaves, the starkness of late autumn tinged with a hint of winter only deepened my sense of isolation. I felt more and more disconnected from the vitality of Life.

I finally arrived home and as I entered my cold, dark apartment, a torrent of anxiety engulfed me. In order to escape the flood tide of emotions that were drowning me, I gulped down all of the pills in that bottle. What happened next is only a dark haze in my memory. I vaguely remember waking up confused and disoriented, surrounded by my dear friend Jimmy, my mother, and my sister.

Apparently, Jimmy was trying to call me for the past few days. Finally, becoming increasingly worried when I didn't respond to his calls, he organized a search party who found me in bed, confused and agitated, lying in my own urine and feces. Jimmy cried when he saw me in such a horrendous state. His love for me was unconditional as he took me into the shower to clean me up. In my delirious state, I must have fallen because I later discovered a contusion on the left side of my rib cage. This seemingly innocuous bruise would have disastrous consequences for me in the weeks that followed.

I was taken to the emergency room and was described as being in an "agitated delirium" by the physician who examined me. After I was stabilized, they transported me back, once again, to the state hospital from which I had been discharged only six weeks earlier. This time I was determined to do whatever I could to avoid another five-week stay. I actively participated in the group therapy sessions and joked with the staff, trying to appear as "normal" as possible, but it was all a charade. Underneath my confident façade was a man teetering on the brink of insanity. My plan worked. After eight days, I was set free, with the recommendation that I follow up at a community mental health clinic near my home.

In the meantime, my mother came up to stay with me. A few days later, I awoke one morning with excruciating chest pain, which was intensified tenfold with each inhalation. Mom took me to the ER where a chest X-ray revealed an abscess in my left lung. Apparently, the contusion to my rib cage that I had sustained a few weeks earlier had also caused bleeding in my lung that had festered and eventually became infected.

Once admitted to the hospital, I was started on intravenous antibiotics and a course of analgesics. However, the infection did not respond to the antibiotics and my lung continued to fill up with more pus. The doctor tried to aspirate the abscess, using a long needle but after several attempts, it became clear that the fluid was coagulated and too thick to be drained using this technique. Then when it seemed things couldn't get worse, they did. The following day, my lung suddenly filled up with so much pus that it became necessary to perform emergency invasive surgery in order to drain the fluid that was by now gravely interfering with my breathing.

They whisked me into the operating room and when the effects of the anesthesia wore off, I found myself in the intensive care unit, a chest tube securely sewn into my left thorax. This tube was connected to a noisy machine that was pumping out any blood or pus that still remained in my lung. I had a full-time private-duty nurse and was on IV morphine. My disturbed emotional state only amplified my pain and overall discomfort.

After spending a day in the ICU, I was then transferred to the medical floor, chest tube and machine attached, where I had to share a small room with a young man who tragically had contracted encephalitis, a serious brain inflammation that can cause permanent brain damage. His family was anxiously hovering around his bedside, making a crowded room even more crowded.

In retrospect, I can see now how my physical and emotional distress prevented me from having empathy for the suffering that this poor man and his family had to endure, because all I thought about was myself feeling trapped, glued to my bed with a tube sticking painfully out of my chest, keeping me attached to that monstrous machine. Finally, the chest tube was removed and soon after that I was well enough to be discharged. The pulmonologist told me that I would have permanent scarring in my lung. This news only added to my misery.

A few days after discharge, I went to the community mental health center that was previously recommended to me, for evaluation and treatment. My physical state, debilitated as it was by all the trauma that I had just gone through, only exacerbated my emotional instability. It was obvious to the therapist at the center that that I was not a candidate for outpatient therapy. Basing his decision on my dramatic response to ECT in the past, he referred me to a psychiatrist who specialized in this therapy. I arrived at her office feeling hollowed out, numb, lifeless, ready to be condemned to the deepest depths of eternal darkness.

As a result of this doctor's skill and compassion, I was admitted into a psychiatric hospital at the end of

December for another round of ECT. After three treatments, the veil of depression, which had shrouded me for so long, began to lift. I was discharged at the beginning of January 2003, not yet ready to return to practice, but feeling hopeful that it would only be a matter of time before I would be able to do so. After several more outpatient ECT treatments, I was finally well enough to begin to make plans to return to practice.

I went to see the psychiatrist whose evaluation would determine whether or not I was able to resume practicing my profession. Initially, he thought I appeared a little bit too anxious. He recommended that I continue psychotherapy before seeing him again. When I returned for another evaluation, he noted that my demeanor was much calmer and my mood was more stable. He then approved my return to practice.

The next challenge was to find a physician who would be willing to come to my office on a regular basis to make sure that I was practicing with "skill and safety." Fortunately, a doctor, with whom I had worked with in the past, was gracious enough to not only agree to monitor me, but also to do the urine drug testing in his office. When the members of the Impaired Physicians Program reviewed his credentials and decided that he was qualified for this position, I was filled with gratitude.

I was amazed at how far I had come in just a few months and thrilled that all of the pieces that would allow me to return to practice were finally coming together. Before I returned to work in February of '03, I treated Jimmy, who had been my rock of Gibraltar through this trying time, to a vacation in Aruba. The warmth and the sunshine in the Caribbean were manna to my soul. I returned back to my practice tanned on the outside, rejuvenated on the inside, and ready to handle *anything* Life had in store for me.

Chapter Eight

Returning to my practice in the beginning of February was like coming home. This was where I belonged. I missed my patients and the feeling had been mutual. In my eyes, the world was sparkling with energy and all of my senses as well as my libido which had deserted me for months, were fully engaged as once again my hypomania was in full swing. I met all of the requirements of the Impaired Physicians Program with ease. The doctor who was monitoring me checked in on a regular basis as required and I reported to his office for urine drug screens twice a week. I also met with my psychiatrist on a monthly basis who sent positive reports to the director of the program.

More good news followed when my monumental legal battle with the insurance companies was finally resolved. After a thorough investigation, an agreement was reached between all parties that was fair and equitable. However, this news was tempered with the pain of having to surrender my New York state medical license because I had not adequately supervised or assumed the many responsibilities that the ownership of these corporations required.

My pulmonologist though was a bearer of good tidings. At my six-week follow-up visit with him, he discovered that there was no trace of scarring or any other damage to my lung on repeat chest X-rays. A blood test that measured my kidney function, which had been in an abnormal range in the years following my nephrectomy, was back to normal for the first time since my surgery. My body was going through such an incredible regenerative process that I was literally awed.

My sense of gratitude for all the blessings that I had received increased my desire to help other people. There was an article in the paper about an organization that sponsored mentoring programs and I contacted the group to get more information. Mentors worked with underprivileged children from broken homes who needed good role models to give them support, caring, and guidance. This organization offered training programs and I happily signed up.

The requirements for being a mentor were simple: a sincere interest in helping children and the willingness to commit to spending one hour a week with them for a minimum of one year. It also required a background check to ensure that there was no criminal history. After being cleared to participate in this program, I was ready to take the next step in becoming a mentor.

I met with the woman who headed the program. After learning that I was a physician, she said that she had the perfect "mentee" for me. Tyler was a sixteen-year-old boy who wanted to be a doctor. Both of his parents were drug addicts and as result, he was taken away from them by the State of Connecticut and placed in a group home with other children who had similar backgrounds.

She arranged for us to meet at his school to make sure we were compatible. I was excited to meet him, although he seemed shy and reticent at out first encounter. He had a welcoming smile and pleasant demeanor. However, during the entire meeting, Tyler avoided looking at me. When the meeting ended, I was convinced that I didn't measure up in his eyes, but his teacher assured me that he was always shy when first meeting people and would warm up once he felt that he could trust me.

Over time, Tyler did let down his guard and I found him to be an amazing young man. I was impressed with his intelligence, strength, and kindness. He was patient with the younger children who lived with him and despite having a busy workload from school, he always managed to find the time to play basketball or other games with them. He also volunteered to help the older children with their homework.

This young man could have followed in his parents' footsteps, becoming a drug addict and wasting his life away, but instead, he decided to fight that temptation and was determined to succeed in life. Tyler never played the role of victim or ever complained about his situation. For all of these reasons, he won my admiration and I was determined to support his goal of becoming a doctor any way I could.

We went to my office and I taught him how to take blood pressure. The sparkle in his eyes and the smile on his face told me that learning how to master this skill meant a lot to him. I also answered all of the questions that he had about what he needed to do in order to get into medical school. Tyler wanted to become a brain surgeon and I knew that he was capable of doing anything that he set his mind to do. I enjoyed our time together and I could tell that the feeling was mutual.

In the end, he became my mentor. By his willingness to strive for excellence in the face of adversity, never complaining or blaming his parents or anyone else for the challenges that he had to face in life, Tyler taught me about courage, faith, fortitude, and forgiveness. I was grateful for the privilege of having known him. It turned out that our relationship was a win-win situation since by reaching out to help someone else, it lifted some of the burdens that I carried in my heart as well.

* * * * *

In April 2003, another momentous event occurred in my life. I met Bobbie, the woman who would change my life forever, even though she thought that our first date was also going to be our last. Over dinner, I was open and honest with her about the problems and issues that I had faced in my life. I wanted her to know from the beginning who I was. Bobbie told me later that I had given her so much information that, although she thought I was a nice guy, she was overwhelmed by learning so much about me so early in our relationship. And who could blame her? Looking back, I have to laugh about my eagerness to take out all the skeletons from my closet on the first date. When we parted company that night, she was determined that this would be the last time she was going to see me. But I persisted until finally, she agreed to another date, which led to another and then another until eventually I succeeded in sweeping her off her feet.

Bobbie and I clicked. When we were together, there was a certain magic, a certain joy, a certain sense of things fitting together just right that flowed between the two of us. She was a strong, self-supportive, and self-assured woman, all winning qualities that attracted me to her from the beginning, not to mention her easygoing manner. Despite barely making it through high school due to the fact that she suffered from dyslexia, Bobbie was very intelligent and determined not to let anything stand in her way of succeeding in life. Her daughter was just a toddler when she was divorced, but Bobbie did not want to rely on her ex- husband for financial support. With no experience in the world of business, she opened up a boutique next to Studio 54 which in its heyday was a famous New York disco. Her store became successful, with clientele including the likes of Andy Warhol.

When Studio 54 shut its doors, she finally had to close her business. Instead of being discouraged and giving up, Bobbie entered into her next business venture by opening up her own restaurant. A lot of responsibilities went along with ownership of this upscale establishment, but she was a quick learner and within a short period of time, the restaurant was packed. When the economy hit bottom, Bobbie had to close this business, but as always, she met the challenge by becoming a successful real estate agent. I admired her ability to always be able to make lemonade out of lemons. Our mutual respect for each other was a major ingredient to the success of our relationship.

Best of all, there was none of the tension or drama that had existed in my previous relationships. We balanced each other out. I brought more discipline and organization to Bobbie's life, and she, in turn, smoothed out my rough edges by teaching me to go with the flow.

That is not to say we never disagree. We have had our share of spats from time to time, but as a friend of mine once said, the sign of a healthy relationship is not how often you fight, but how long it takes you to make up. Usually our disagreements have been caused by my sometimes fiery temperament or my belief that, as my high school gym teacher, Mr. Benjamin, always liked to say, I am not always right but I am never wrong. Typically, after one of our quarrels, I look deeply into to my soul, ponder what I have said, and, after a short period of introspection, I apologize. Somehow we always find the humor in the situation and dissolve into a chorus of giggles and hugs. We never hold grudges, which I believe is also a sign of a healthy relationship. From my experience I have learned that lack of forgiveness, anger, and biting sarcasm are death knolls to any relationship.

Even Mom approved of Bobbie. Granted, I had never needed her approval of my other relationships, but it was still nice to receive her approbation. My mother had her own unique reason as to why my other relationships had failed. She would always say, "Alan, you'll never meet anyone as nice as your mother." But this time, Mom had to admit that I had finally met the woman who could measure up to her exacting standards. For the time being, harmony ruled in my life.

* * * * *

However, all too soon the calm waters were disturbed by another major storm. In early summer of 2003, blood tests and MRIs revealed that my mother's cancer was spreading. While the oncologist started her on more aggressive chemotherapy, I insisted that she now needed to come up to my office for intravenous treatments at least twice a week.

Then, in mid-August, everything started to snowball when I received a call from my mother's neighbor who told me that Mom had been in bed all day, unable to keep down any fluids. I spoke to my mother, and as always, she put up a strong front, but I could tell that there was something wrong. Once again, I refused to accept that my mother was going to die and I was determined to do whatever I could to prevent this.

I went to her house and was shocked to find her in such a fragile, weakened state. However, assuming my role as physician, I started an IV in an attempt to replace the fluids that she could not take orally. It filled me with panic to see this woman who had always been a pillar of strength, lying there so helplessly. She seemed to respond to the IV fluids so I went home, still hopeful that the worst was over.

My unrealistic expectations were quickly shattered. The next day I got a call from my cousin who told me that her condition was critical. Mom now required immediate hospitalization. I rushed to the hospital emergency room and saw her lying on a stretcher being examined by the oncologist, her face distorted by pain, her eyes barely open. "I did the best I could," the doctor told me, "but there is nothing more that I can offer. I am so sorry."

Holding my mother's hand, I choked back tears as I whispered how much I loved her. Later on, I found out that my mom had been in a lot of pain over the past month, as the cancer had metastasized to her bones. But she had hid her suffering from me because she was concerned about the effect that this information would have on my emotional well-being. After she was transferred onto the medical floor, various members of our family and friends took turns sitting by her bedside. Silence settled over the room, broken only by an occasional sob. Words were not necessary. Mom knew how much they loved her.

Throughout her life, my mother had always made it a point to play an active role in their lives, remembering everybody's birthday, sending cards and calling to send her love and good wishes. Mom was always one of the first to appear at the hospital to celebrate the birth of her grandchildren, grandnieces, and nephews. My mother always tried to find out the hobbies and interests of her relatives, so that she could bone up on these topics and engage them in intelligent conversations. She learned about the favorite music and movies of the younger members of the family, whom she often surprised by knowing the name of their favorite rap singer or actor.

In their younger years, her grandchildren were rabid Harry Potter fans and Mom took them to Barnes and Noble for the midnight release of the latest book. When Staci fell in love with Cabbage Patch dolls years ago, my parents took her to the special place where these babies were "born" so that she could pick out her own doll, which filled their granddaughter with delight from head to toe. These were only some of the ways that Mom showed her love and devotion for her family.

I knew that it was my mother's time to leave and finally surrendered to that painful fact. Mom was at peace knowing that Bobbie would be there to love and comfort me. Little did Bobbie know then that her love for me would be tested only six short months later when I would again fall into the bottomless pit of depression.

But for this last, long moment, my mother was the center of my life. I held her hand and stroked her forehead as I told her that she could let go, that there was nothing to fear. Even though her eyes were closed, and she was too weak to speak, I knew that she heard me. Trying to ease some of the pain in both of our hearts, I jokingly said, "Dad is waiting for you on the other side and you know how he hates to be kept waiting," at which she smiled weakly, an acknowledgment that brought me both joy and sorrow. At last I kissed her good-bye, knowing this would be last time that I would see her.

My sister, who throughout her life had endured a tumultuous relationship with my mother, did not want Mom to die alone. Determined to stay by her bedside until the very end, Kathi remained with her until the early morning hours when Mom passed away. My heart was paralyzed with grief, but I buried that pain deeply within the recesses of my psyche. There it would grow until it would have to finally break through to the surface in order to let the anguish flow freely. When I finally did acknowledge her loss, this sorrow would send me spiraling down into a world of utter darkness.

At Mom's funeral, I started the eulogy for her with three words, words she had so often heard her father repeat when she was a child: "*Zein a mensch.*" This is a Yiddish expression that, like so many others is difficult to translate, but I will do the best I can because it describes the essence of the character of my mother. "*Zein a mensch.*" Be a person of substance, a person with manners, dignity, strength, and conviction. My mother certainly embodied all of these qualities, always carrying herself with elegance and grace. Despite our differences, I had a deep respect and admiration for her. My daughter, niece, and nephew also gave their own eulogies for the grandmother whom they loved and adored.

Later, I thought to myself how to the very end, Mom's thoughts were about me. My birthday was coming up in a few weeks and she had ordered tickets to a Broadway play as her gift to me. These tickets still had not arrived and lying on her deathbed, in the depths of her pain and misery, she told her next-door neighbor to check the mail to make sure that I would get her birthday gift. It would be a long time before I would use these tickets. The memories attached to this gift were too painful for me to endure.

After the funeral, we returned to my mother's apartment where my sister and I started to "sit *Shiva*," which, in the Jewish religion, is a period of mourning. Family, friends, and loved ones came to visit us to express their condolences and support. Although I appreciated the love and support of people who came to visit, I felt as though my mother's small apartment, where I had grown up and, more recently, had shared many special moments with her, was a sanctuary and that they were invading the sanctity of this space. Maybe this was because many of the people who came to visit were friends of my sister who thrived on their support and company.

In contrast, I craved privacy and sought refuge in my mother's bedroom, where I read and meditated. After this period of mourning ended, my sister was upset with me since she felt that we had not mourned together. I explained that our different ways of mourning should be respected; she needed the company of her friends for comfort and I needed privacy to commune with my thoughts and feelings. It took a while, but she finally understood my point of view.

Adjusting to life without my parents came as a shock to my system. Even though I was close to fifty years old, I still felt like an orphan. Together, Mom and Dad had played many roles in my formative years. They were a source of strength and wisdom, a haven for love and understanding. We had shared an intimate bond that is unique to parents and children. Although I felt a void in my heart when my father passed away, Mom's presence in my life had kept me tethered to my roots, in part, because Dad's spirit continued to live through her.

My mom's apartment, which was now my main connection to my past, would soon need to be sold. As we closed the door to her home, a chapter in my life closed forever. My grief was so intense that I also sealed shut the door to my heart in order to protect me from an almost excruciating pain. Life would go on, but in a fundamental way, it would never be quite the same again.

Bobbie and I returned to her home, where I was now living. Our love continued to thrive. Her compassion and support nurtured my soul. I was happy that she and Mom had the opportunity to get to know each other. I could only offer memories of my dad to Bobbie, but the personal connection that she had with my mother helped her to understand the extent of my loss. Both of her parents were still living and although she couldn't fully identify with the deep grief that I was experiencing, she did her best to comfort me.

When the end of January 2004 arrived, I assumed that my grief had become more manageable. But my return to Mom's apartment for the first time since sitting *Shiva* in August served as a brutal reminder that the pain of her loss was still buried deeply within my heart. Still, since it was time to pack up her things in preparation for the sale of what had once been our home, Bobbie and I met my sister there to begin what all of us recognized would be a difficult process.

The collage of memories that confronted me as I entered her apartment nullified my ability to be of any help in this endeavor. Numbly, I sifted through her collection of photographs, vainly attempted to pack her clothes, and blankly stared at all the pots and pans that had cooked so many great meals, aware of an overwhelming impulse to flee. I knew that I had to leave because the pain was too insufferable. "I'm going Kathi," I said. "Sorry, but I can't take it." And then, before she had a chance to respond, I took Bobbie's hand and made a mad dash to the car.

By the time we returned home, it was evening. All I wanted to do was to numb the agony that was tearing my heart apart. At first I thought I could seek refuge in sleep, but I was too agitated to drift off into the world of dreams without some help so I took one tranquilizer. But when I awoke in the morning, my mind was held prisoner by the iron grip of fear. I knew that my urine test for drugs, which I had been doing on a regular basis since I had returned to practice, would now be positive and this would jeopardize my ability to maintain my medical license. The fear of losing my license coupled with the intense grief that I had buried since my mother's funeral now rose explosively to the surface, plummeting me into a world of desperation that would lead me to three separate psychiatric hospitalizations and ten rounds of ECT within a span of thirty days.

* * * * *

I had patients scheduled for that morning but since I was so overwhelmed by grief and anxiety, return to my practice was not possible. Fortunately, Bobbie quickly found a doctor to take care of my patients.

Once again the recurrent refrain of winter was playing in the background as I slid into a state of deep despair. In order to numb my feelings, I started to medicate myself with alcohol and tried to hide my alcohol abuse from Bobbie. But when I started to travel down the road of binge drinking, this secret could no longer be concealed with the result that I was admitted to Yale New Haven Psychiatric Hospital on February 6, 2004.

In his admission notes, my psychiatrist wrote that I had experienced "one week of worsening dysphoria [anxiety/depression], anergia [low energy], decreased activities of daily living and inability to work," and that I was "stable until one week prior to admission." It was during this hospitalization that I found a new path for my life, setting me on the road to recovery from my lifetime battle with depression. After a careful review of my clinical history, my psychiatrist changed my longstanding diagnosis of major depression to Bipolar 2 Disorder.

In order to understand why this change in diagnosis was such a turning point in my life, it is important to give more information on the spectrum of bipolar disorders and what makes them distinct from major depression. Bipolar 1, also known as manic-depression, is associated with a period of mania that is characterized by the following signs and symptoms: increased energy, rapid speech, euphoric mood, grandiosity, racing thoughts, the need for little sleep, poor judgment, spending sprees, increased sexual drive, abuse of drugs, particularly alcohol and sleeping medications, denial that anything is wrong, impulsivity, and, in its most severe form, frank psychosis. There is also a depressive phase that mimics the clinical picture of major depression. Symptoms often seen in this phase include: markedly diminished interest or pleasure in all, or almost all activities most of the day, nearly every day, chronic depressed mood, significant weight loss or gain, insomnia or sleeping more than normal, feelings of worthlessness, excessive guilt, inability to concentrate, fatigue, and recurrent thoughts of death and suicide.

The signs and symptoms of the "hypomania" associated with bipolar 2 are similar to the manic symptoms seen in bipolar 1, but not as pronounced and are of shorter duration. Bipolar 2 Disorder is also associated with severe depressive episodes. In major depression, there are no signs or symptoms of any form of mania. However the depression common to all three conditions can be equally devastating.

The depression associated with bipolar 2 is often misdiagnosed as major depression because the hypomanic symptoms are often subtle and therefore are easily missed by physicians. But at times, even the more overt symptoms of the mania associated with bipolar 1 go undetected or unreported by the patient. As a result, studies have shown that as many as 40 percent of both inpatients and outpatients diagnosed with depression are subsequently found to have bipolar disorders. In addition, the prevalence of this psychiatric disorder that was previously believed to affect two million Americans, actually affects closer to ten million individuals when both bipolar disorders are considered.

Patients like me, with Bipolar 2 Disorder are more frequently misdiagnosed with major depression than those with bipolar 1 for two reasons: 1) Often patients feel remarkably well when hypomanic, and are, therefore, unlikely to spontaneously report these episodes. 2) Patients with bipolar 2, in contrast to bipolar 1, do not present with any psychotic symptoms, which allows them to fly under the radar screen of clinical detection. Both of these factors were true in my case.

A thorough case history, as well as an in-depth knowledge of Bipolar 2 Disorder, is vital in making the proper diagnosis, particularly since the consequences of misdiagnosing this illness can sometimes mean the difference between life and death. Functional impairment and suicide are substantially greater in bipolar disorders than in major depression. Lifetime risk of suicide attempts among patients with bipolar disorders ranges from 25 percent to 50 percent, while estimates of completed suicide are between 10 to 15 percent.

In addition, the antidepressants used to treat major depression are usually ineffective in the treatment of bipolar disorders and some studies suggest that they can actually trigger mania. Another class of drugs, known as mood stabilizers, is used in the treatment of bipolar disorders. Furthermore, if this mood disorder is not properly diagnosed and treated, the illness can increase in frequency and severity. This is what happened to me. I had been on many different antidepressants throughout my life, but nonetheless my episodes of depression continued unabated.

At first, I was reluctant to accept his diagnosis of Bipolar 2 Disorder. However, looking back on my history of depression that had plagued me for over thirty years, it was apparent that I did suffer from this problem. In retrospect, it was clear that after every depressive episode, I had an upswing in energy and a significant improvement in my mood, enjoying a tremendous exhilaration that I attributed to how one would naturally feel after recovering from the depths of despair.

There were other hypomanic symptoms as well. Following my recovery from these episodes of depression, I would feel refreshed and ready to go after only five or six hours of sleep. After each episode of depression, my libido, which had been dormant for so long, would spring into action. My impulsivity, which caused me to rush headlong into relationships and marriages, was also a typical symptom of hypomania. Even though, thankfully, I never suffered from the psychosis associated with the mania of bipolar 1, my life had nevertheless been turned upside down as a result of the episodes of hypomania that I had experienced for the past three decades.

There were other clues in my clinical history that also pointed to this diagnosis. The depression associated with bipolar disorder is often triggered or exacerbated by winter which was consistent with my long history of depression. In addition, the age of onset of the first depressive episode is critical in making the diagnosis of bipolar disorder. If the onset of the first depression occurs before the age of twenty-five, it is very likely that the underlying diagnosis is bipolar mood disorder. This was also consistent with my history of depression, since my first episode occurred when I was twenty. If I had been correctly diagnosed and treated at that time, it would have greatly improved my long-term prognosis and likely would have prevented my many episodes of depression that required over the course of my life twelve psychiatric hospitalizations and over thirty ECT treatments.

Once correctly diagnosed, I was started on a medication called Lamictal® which is an anticonvulsant that also acts as mood stabilizer, and is highly effective in the treatment of Bipolar 2 Disorder. This drug has fewer side effects than lithium, which was first used for the treatment of manic-depressive illness. In addition, recent studies suggest that Lamictal®, unlike lithium, can also act to prevent the depressive phase associated with this disorder. This medication does have one potentially serious side effect; a severe skin disorder known as Stevens-Johnson syndrome. The risk of developing this side effect can be minimized however by slowly building up to a therapeutic dose, although there is the disadvantage of having to wait four to six weeks before the optimal dose is reached.

Since I was still suffering from severe depression, a course of ECT was also instituted. After three treatments, the psychiatrist's notes revealed that I "appeared to have a robust response with a return of mood to a near euthymic [normal] state." I was then discharged on February 13 with follow-up plans to continue outpatient ECT treatments.

However, my recovery was only temporary. The underlying stresses in my life and the psychic wounds caused by my relationship with my mother still had not totally healed. I had come to the fork in the road where ECT would no longer be an effective treatment for my recurrent episodes of depression. Until these issues were resolved, they would continue to trigger my battle with this illness.

As a consequence, when I returned home, panic and dread still plagued me. Returning to my practice was clearly not yet possible. Without anything to provide me with a sense of purpose, I drifted into a world of all-consuming, unceasing anxiety, a condition that in my unbalanced state of mind, only alcohol could assuage. This was highly out of character for me since my drinking was usually limited to an occasional glass of wine at dinner or a beer from time to time during the summer. However, having entered still another world of emotional chaos, I abused alcohol and Ativan® and paid dearly for my actions.

At first after my return home, as soon as Bobbie left for work in the morning, I walked to the nearest bar, a necessary step since she had now taken all of the alcohol out of the house. By 10 a.m., fully intoxicated, I would somehow find my way home in time to sober up before Bobbie returned home from work.

I then turned to Ativan® to soothe the anxiety that was strangling me. My mental state quickly unraveled and could no longer be kept hidden from her. I was again admitted to Yale New Haven Psychiatric Hospital on February 16. This time, I received four additional ECT treatments and "improved fairly dramatically clinically" but in truth, as I was soon to discover, my sanity was hanging by thread. When I was discharged on February 26, the plan was to taper off the ECT and continue maintenance treatments and psychotherapy on an outpatient basis. I was also advised not to return to work. However, the problems that had triggered these hospitalizations still haunted me. I was given a prescription for Seroquel®, a non-narcotic sedative meant to quell my anxiety, a drug that I promptly abused. My heavy drinking also continued unabated. This dangerous combination only exacerbated my emotional instability and led me into a haze of utter confusion and chaos.

By March 2, 2004, extremely depressed and withdrawn, I was again readmitted to Yale. I began another course of ECT for a total of ten treatments, which, except for some mild disorientation and short-term memory loss, I tolerated well. And again, there was some improvement in my condition. After one week, I was discharged with a referral to an outpatient treatment program. My dose of Lamictal® was also increased, yet was still far from a therapeutic level.

My emotional roller coaster was starting to take its toll on Bobbie, fraying her nerves and stretching her patience to the breaking point. Even so, she did not give up, in part because she had some understanding of my illness since a close member of her family had suffered from depression for most of their adult life. Also, the memories of the love and joy that we had shared were too precious for her to abandon. At one point, I was worried that she would leave me. To demonstrate her commitment to our relationship, she promised to marry me once I recovered. But we were both aware that I was still going to have to do a lot of work before this could happen.

As recommended, I went to the treatment program. Not surprisingly, I wanted out as soon as I got there, mainly because this place was a long way from home and I needed to be closer to Bobbie. When I called and begged her to come get me, she agreed, but with one stipulation: I would have to be admitted to Silver Hill Hospital for treatment. I agreed, and the next day she came to pick me up. Unfortunately, it took more time than expected to make arrangements for my admission. During the days that followed, I drifted back into my pattern of drug and alcohol abuse and as a result, it wouldn't be long before I ached to jump into abyss of death in order to escape from the unrelenting pain and misery that were smothering me.

Chapter Nine

Finally, I was admitted to Silver Hill Hospital on March 22, 2004. It was a blessing to be back in the serene ambiance of this facility, but I was in no condition to take advantage of all the comforts that it had to offer me. Drug and alcohol abuse combined with my unrelenting anxiety had left me hollow, dead inside, wanting nothing more than to lose consciousness forever. My mind was incapacitated and it was a struggle to speak more than two-word sentences. I barely participated in the group therapy activities. My quick wit and sense of humor had deserted me long ago. This total absence of feeling was intolerable and I thought of death as the only solution to relieve my suffering.

After a week of this, I solidified plans to commit suicide as soon as I was discharged. I would, I told myself, overdose on sleeping pills and sedatives washed down with a quart of vodka. In order not to alert anyone to my plans, I put on as good a face as possible, especially in front of Bobbie, intent on convincing her that everything was under control and that I was, in fact, much better.

That night, while speaking on the phone to a friend, I hinted that I was planning to take my life. "Think of Bobbie," she told me. "Do you know how much she loves you? Do you know how much this is going to hurt her?" Suddenly, the wall of ice that had frozen my heart melted and, for the first time in months, a flood of tears poured down my cheeks. I didn't want to hurt the woman I loved, but it was too agonizing for me to go on living.

Hanging up the phone, I ran into my room and fell to my knees. "Please help me! Show me a way out of this darkness!" I cried out to God from the deepest depths of my being. I had been on a spiritual path for a long time, praying and meditating on a daily basis, but it wasn't until my unconditional surrender to God that the door to my ultimate healing and happiness finally opened.

The next day, while I was lying in bed, hiding from the world, a nurse who was always caring, brought me a book entitled, *Angelspeake a Guide – How to Talk with Your Angels,* co-authored by Barbara Mark and Trudy Griswold. This book was short, but very sweet. It gave instructions on how to speak to your angels by using "The Four Fundamentals" and "The Seven Steps." Each chapter included letters that were written by a variety of people to their angelic guides.

As I read the loving words of the angels in response to those letters, I felt surrounded by their presence and my heart filled with hope. Immediately, I began to write letter after letter to my angels, imploring them for their assistance and guidance. Miraculously, within just a few days of intense prayer and supplication, I began my journey out of the darkness and into the light, filled with a sense of peace and calm that had been absent from my life for so long.

Slowly, I began to dig my way out of the tomb of gloom in which I had been buried for what felt like eons. Each morning, I dragged myself out of bed and exercised at the gym located on the grounds of Silver Hill. Before long, I was able to enjoy all the comforts that this place offered, including the luxury of having my own room, which provided me with peace and privacy.

Since this was not a locked unit, I was able to leave the building and walk the grounds. With my appetite back in full force, I began to look forward to my trips to the cafeteria. There was a wide variety of food, served in buffet style and I savored every mouthful. Hospital policy also allowed guests to eat with patients in the dining room, which was prohibited at the other places where I had been hospitalized. A sense of normalcy returned to my world whenever Bobbie joined me for dinner.

I also forged friendships with my fellow "inmates." There was Ann, a pleasant and talkative middle-aged woman who was withdrawing from an inadvertent overdose of the potent tranquilizer, Xanax®. She had used this drug as a way of coping with the stressful life of being a busy housewife and raising three precocious teenage daughters. Her withdrawal from this drug was slow and painful. At first, like me, she had great difficulty in maintaining any meaningful conversation. As both of us slowly came back to the land of the living, we found that we had a lot in common. Another factor that increased my fondness for Ann was her high opinion of Bobbie. The two had met on visiting day, and once, after Bobbie left, Ann told me that she was "the greatest!" I couldn't have agreed more!

There was also Karen, a young woman who was an assistant executive at an Ivy League university whose withdrawal from alcohol had created huge gaps in her memory. To compensate for this, she carried a pad and pen everywhere she went and wrote down the schedule for all the group therapy sessions as well as other activities on the floor. A gentle, sweet, soft-spoken woman, Karen also became one of my exercise buddies. Fortunately, by the time of her discharge, the harmful effects of the alcohol had resolved and there was a great improvement in her memory and cognition.

As my condition continued to get better, I asked Bobbie to bring my guitar to the hospital. Every night, after visiting hours were over, my fellow patients and I would gather in the TV room and sink into the leather couches and comfortable chairs. As I played songs familiar to all of us, we would join in singing raucous choruses of *Hey Mr. Tambourine Man* and *Brown-Eyed Girl* with so much energy that even Bob Dylan and Van Morrison would have been proud. We were having so much fun that once one of the aides thought that we were partaking in recreational drugs, which was definitely not the case! So many close bonds were formed between us that each time someone was discharged, there was a flurry of exchange of e-mail addresses and phone numbers.

Now that I was fully alive and engaged in life, it was time to for me to face one of the issues that was dragging me down the road of self-destruction: the fear of losing my medical license. I had entangled my self-identity in my role as a physician and if that role was taken away from me, I worried that my sense of self, my purpose for being, would dissolve. My license had been suspended because of the events of the past few months and I knew that it would be an uphill battle to have it reinstated.

The answer to my dilemma came in the form of a gentleman named Desmond, who was one of the psychiatric aides that worked on the floor. He was a soft-spoken man with a melodic, soothing Jamaican accent who said to me, "Are you Alan Cohen the doctor, or Alan Cohen the man?" Desmond's words affected me profoundly and caused a major shift in my psychology. Without hesitation, I embraced Alan Cohen the man. I would still try to get my license back, but I surrendered the outcome to God. I felt at peace knowing that when one door closed, another one would open.

On April 2, I was ready to be discharged. The rush of energy and intense, exhilarating joy that had possessed me after many of my previous hospitalizations was absent. I felt balanced, calm, and serene thanks in part to the Lamictal®. My dose of this medication would still have to be increased over the next few weeks, but I was already on the road to wellness. Bobbie would also need time to heal from the hell that I had put her through. Our relationship required the time and space to recover from the trauma of the last few months, but I was certain that with love and patience it would be stronger than ever before.

I was now ready to tackle a major cause of my many episodes of depression: the relationship with my mother. Although I had made some progress in that area, more work needed to be done in order to heal the deep-seated wounds that still remained hidden in my psyche. Trudy Griswold would be instrumental in leading me to the remarkable individual who would guide me through this process.

* * * * *

When I returned home from Silver Hill Hospital, my number one priority was to stay healthy: mentally, emotionally, and physically. To this end, I attended the outpatient treatment program for professionals that was previously recommended to me. I also saw a psychologist on a weekly basis and my psychiatrist who monitored my response to the Lamictal®, slowly increasing it to the therapeutic dose. Regular exercise was also an integral part of my recovery plan. For intellectual stimulation, I took a course in acupuncture that reinforced my idea of the importance of the mind-body connection. The study of this ancient Eastern healing art also gave me another vantage point in which to view health and wellness.

I would like to give a brief summary of the history and theory of acupuncture because it has been an important tool that has helped in my recovery. Acupuncture dates back to ancient China during the Shang dynasty in 1766 B.C. According to traditional Chinese medicine, the body has a series of channels, known as meridians, that exist on an energetic level and run from head to toe, connecting to the various physical organs. There are a series of thousands of acupuncture points throughout the body that make up these meridians and there are some interesting theories as to how these acupuncture points were discovered.

As in many other fields of medicine, the power of observation was important. One theory is that acupuncture points were possibly discovered way back in the Stone Age. It is thought that stone knives and sharp tools were used at that time to relieve pain and disease such as lancing boils, and these primitive people may have also noted sensations or changes in other parts of the body subsequent to treatment with these tools. Later in history, warriors in battle who were hit by arrows may have sometimes noticed conduction of their pain to other areas of the body. In the Middle Ages, monks noticed the movement of energy from one part of the body to another when they meditated. Over the centuries, through scientific application and observation, these energy movements were painstakingly noted and the channel system was gradually elaborated into the intricate, fascinating meridian system that is now used in traditional Chinese medicine.

An underlying principle in Chinese medicine is the theory of Chi, which is synonymous with the vital force discussed in homeopathy. It is the body's innate healing capacity. Chi is more of a concept than an actual physical entity. It is what flows along the meridians. The disruption or blockage of the flow of Chi results in disease. The aim of treatment is to insert needles into specific acupuncture points, which then allows Chi to flow smoothly along the meridians and other channels resulting in wellness on all levels: mental, emotional and physical.

A fundamental tenet of traditional Chinese medicine states that there is an intimate connection between the individual and Nature. According to this ancient healing art, Nature in all of its elements, fire, air, water, and earth has a direct effect on all the meridians and, in turn, on all the corresponding organs connected to these meridians. The elements also shape our mental and emotional makeup. This is consistent with the theory of quantum physics that postulates the existence, on a subatomic level, of a Cosmic Web, interweaving and interconnecting all life on planet earth.

Another important principle of traditional Chinese medicine involves the concept of yin and yang. The yin is the feminine aspect of Nature and has corresponding qualities such as cold, dark, and wet. The yang refers to the masculine polarity of Nature and it also has particular characteristics such as hot, bright, and dry. Indeed, according to Chinese philosophy, yin-yang represents all of existence in its infinite forms. The balance of the yin and yang in both mind and body leads to health and wholeness.

While I was taking this course on acupuncture, I had a series of treatments. After each session, I felt peaceful and yet more energetic, which together produced an overall improvement in my sense of well-being. Since the course ended, I have had periodic acupuncture treatments, usually during the change of seasons. This has been quite effective in helping me maintain my level of wellness. I have given only a brief explanation of this fascinating field of healing and for those who want to know more, I recommend the book *Between Heaven And Earth: A Guide To Chinese Medicine*, by Harriet Beinfield, L.Ac., and Efrem Korngold, L.Ac., O.M.D.

At the end of April, I went to a workshop in New York City given by Trudy Griswold, who had co-authored the book *Angelspeake* that had been so instrumental in my healing. I wanted to express my profound gratitude to her as well as share my experience with the other attendees at the conference. After the workshop was over, Trudy thanked me for telling my story, one which she said had profoundly affected everyone in the class as was evidenced by the hush that fell over the room while I was speaking. It turned out that Trudy lived only a short distance from our home. A few weeks after the workshop, I went to her office for several sessions that were very enlightening. She also introduced me to Dr. Akhter Ahsen, a remarkable and brilliant man who was a pioneer in the field of eidetic imagery, an innovative form of psychotherapy.

Dr. Ahsen, whose Ph.D. is in psychology, had begun researching the field of eidetic imagery back in the 1970s. The author of over thirty books on this field of psychology, he has also written numerous articles on this topic. Since this therapy was so instrumental in healing the wound in my psyche that had been caused by my often painful relationship with my mother, I think that it is important to give a brief explanation of this topic.

The word "eidetic" is connected to the Greek word "*eidie*," meaning a clear visual image. An eidetic is a specific kind of mental image different from the dream, daydream, or guided fantasy in that it is fixed and consistently reproducible. Neurological proof of these images was found by Dr. Wilder Penfield. He discovered that touching selected points in the temporal cortex of his patients resulted in vivid recall of the eidetic images, which, in turn, re-created past experiences of the events and conflicts in a person's life with remarkable clarity and detail.

Dr. Ahsen made a breakthrough discovery in this field when he found that these images were more than simply visual. They had other components, both somatic and emotional, as well as having an underlying meaning. According to Ahsen, the eidetic image emerges at points where there is conflict in the mind, but unlike ordinary images, they preserve the full memory of the conflict. More importantly, he found that these images appear to be associated with the parents.

In order to identify the exact nature of these conflicts, Ahsen devised the Eidetics Parents Test or EPT, which consists of thirty basic images. He pointed out that, although in the test, the parents appear as two separated and insulated images in the patient's mind, the most important attribute is how the parents interact; that is, how they tend to deal with each other, the patient, as well as other members of the family.

To demonstrate this theory, Dr. Ahsen told me to imagine my parents standing in front of me. When I had done so, he asked which parent was on the left. Without hesitation, I told him that my mother was on the left. According to his research, if both parents had played an equal role in my life, then I should have seen my father on the left. However, seeing my mother on the left indicated that she was the dominant parent. Although it is beyond the scope of the book to explain the reasoning behind this fact, it was true that with just one image and with only a brief history of the relationship that I had had with my mother, he was able to discern the domineering role that she had played in shaping my psyche.

Dr. Ahsen then asked me to imagine to myself in the apartment that I lived in when I was two years old. Immediately, I saw myself on my father's lap listening to him patiently explain to me that we needed to move to a larger apartment in order to make room for my newborn sister. According to Ahsen, this meant that my father treated me with love and respect as I was growing up, which was true.

Next, he asked me to see myself in that apartment in relation to where my mom was located. Without missing a beat, I clearly saw myself as an infant and she was standing over my crib. From this he deduced, correctly, that throughout my life, my mother perceived me to be a helpless infant, and as a result she always wanted to keep me in an "egg," that is, under her protective control.

Again, without knowing my full history, Dr. Ahsen hit the nail on the head regarding the crux of the conflict within the relationship between my mother and me. In addition, he said that the emotional trauma caused by moving from the security of my home, coupled with the need to share my parents' attention with my sister, also contributed to my long history of anxiety and depression.

During the sessions that followed, as one part of the therapy, he had me recall the positive, loving memories that I had with my mother. Later on in the course of my treatment when he re-administered the test, I consistently saw my father on the left and my mother on the right. With their reversal to this position, there was a profound healing of the wound in my psyche caused by the difficult relationship that I had experienced with my mother.

Throughout my life, although I had made some improvement with different types of psychotherapy from inner child work to cognitive behavior, I found eidetic imagery to be the most effective in healing the root cause of my lifelong struggle with depression. I have given only a brief introduction to the field of eidetic imagery. For those who want more information on this vital topic, I suggest that you read the book by Ann T. Dolan, M.D., a student of Dr. Ahsen's, called *Imagery of Phobias, Anxiety States and Other Symptom Complexes in Akhter Ahsen's Image Psychology*.

I also worked on healing my relationship with Bobbie, the first woman in my life to love me unconditionally. In the first month following my discharge from Silver Hill, things were a little rocky between us. We needed time to get reacquainted after being separated for two months during my illness. But her willingness to stand by me during my worst of times deepened my love and admiration for her. In some ways, this time of tribulation had strengthened our bonds. As the weeks passed, I realized that I wanted nothing more than to marry her. We talked about getting married in another year or two in order to give me time to heal from the long ordeal that I had just been through.

Mending my relationship with Staci was also a priority for me. While I was in the hospital, she called Bobbie, upset that no one was telling her what was going on with me. Even though I had been back in her life since 1992, just as she turned eleven, Staci had always been kept in the dark about my battle with depression, but now she wanted to know everything about my problem. After discharge, I met with my daughter and for the first time, filled her in on my life from the time that I left her when she was just three years old to the present.

It was, perhaps, naïve of me to think that once I poured out my heart to her, we would be closer than ever before in our lives. When this did not happen, I was upset and disappointed. Fortunately, my therapist helped me to understand Staci's hesitancy to fully embrace me. She said that my daughter might have felt overwhelmed by the vast amount of information that I had given her, information that no doubt she would need time to process. It was, she said, also entirely possible that the hurt and anger Staci must have felt about me leaving her when she was so young made it difficult for her to let down her guard now and fully trust me. Either way, I resigned myself to the fact that it was going to take time, love, and patience to rebuild our relationship and I was more than willing to do whatever I could to make this happen.

* * * * *

A few weeks in later at the end of April, Bobbie told me that she was in love, but at that moment in time it wasn't me who was the object of her adoration. As it turned out though, I had nothing to worry about. While surfing the Internet for a new mail box, she came across an animal rescue Web site where she found the picture of an adorable, ten-pound scruffy dog named Gracie, who was in foster care in nearby Westchester County. Bobbie pleaded with me to come with her to see Gracie.

I agreed and we also took Chelsea along, our other rescue dog, to see if she would get along with Gracie. They became fast friends. Suddenly we were a two-dog family. Fozzie, our black and white cat also made the adjustment to having another dog in the house although he made it clear that he was still the boss.

In the past, lapdogs had never appealed to me. The thought of walking this little dog in public was damaging to my "macho" image. I needed to have a big dog, a "man's" dog. As a result, when I first moved to Connecticut, Lulu, a seventy-pound, gentle, loving yellow Lab, was my constant companion.

But over time, Gracie grew on me. This little dog, whom I christened a "doodle," because she was a mix of dachshund and poodle, craved my constant attention. Every time I sat down, she would dive into my lap begging for my love, which I couldn't resist giving to her. We also had this little game whereby each time I went upstairs, she would run ahead of me, jump on the bed, and lay on her back so that I could scratch her belly. This pup was also a natural-born comedienne, which only endeared her to me more. I truly believe that Gracie, so aptly named, was given to me by the grace of God because she has brought immeasurable joy into my life.

As the days passed, I still planned on getting my license reinstated. The lawyer, who was representing me, advised that I continue my treatment program for at least six months before approaching the Department of Public Health with a request for the reinstatement of my medical license. I agreed and was determined to continue my strategy for wellness. In my heart, I was willing to surrender the outcome of the department's decision to God. My faith and trust in His wisdom was a source of solace and hope for me.

During this time, my relationship with Bobbie also strengthened and comforted me. She was my best friend, my confidante, my lover, my muse. Although we had intended on getting married next year, we no longer wanted to wait that long and decided to move up the date.

Bobbie was excited about this, but she was also concerned that it might be too soon for me to make such a big commitment. She thought that I still needed time to heal since I had only been out of the hospital for a few months. I assured her that I was ready.

We made plans to get married in July and started our search for the "perfect" place to hold our celebration. Since we both had been married before, we didn't want anything too formal. We were looking for a venue that offered comfort and warmth, tinged with a hint of elegance. It didn't take too long to find exactly what we wanted. It was a quaint inn tucked away in the woods on the banks of a river.

Wedding invitations went out a week later and we eagerly looked forward to exchanging vows in front of our close friends and family. I felt a twinge of remorse that my mom would not be there to share in my joy, but I was comforted in knowing she would always be with me in my heart.

As the day approached, I became more and more anxious. "What am I doing?" I said to myself. "Are you crazy, getting married AGAIN?!" were the words that constantly crisscrossed my mind. Since this fear of marriage had nothing to do with Bobbie, whom I loved and adored, I realized that it was the ghosts of my marriages past that were haunting me.

Given that the underlying foundation our relationship

was based on trust and honesty, I had to share my feelings with Bobbie, who was patient and loving as always. She said that if I wanted to postpone the wedding that was okay with her. Her kindness and concern for my well-being touched me deeply. I knew that my love for Bobbie was stronger than my fear as I reaffirmed my desire to marry her.

At the end of July, the day arrived that would mark the new beginning of our lives together. We reserved the inn at a time in which there would be no other events going on. This gave us the privacy and intimacy that we wanted for our ceremony and celebration. On a warm, sunny, summer day, the altar was set up outside with the river serving as a backdrop.

As soon as the ceremony began, all of my doubts and fears melted away in the summer heat. Peace, joy, and gratitude surrounded me. I knew without a doubt that this marriage was the best thing that could ever have happened to me. Encircled by our dear friends and family, we exchanged wedding vows accompanied by the soft, soothing music of flute and guitar playing in the background. It was a magical day.

Soon it was October, and six months had passed since my discharge from the hospital. It was now time to try to get my license reinstated. My lawyer approached the Department of Public Health with a letter from my psychiatrist stating that I had "followed my treatment plan with excellent cooperation" and that I had done "exceptionally well in therapy …(my) mental status had remained stable." My attorney tried to work out an agreement with the department that would allow me to return to practice, but the officials were adamant and agreed to nothing short of the revocation of my license.

I was disappointed and perplexed as to the reason for the department's extreme stubbornness. It was well known that physicians suffer from a higher rate of mood disorders than the general population, yet many of them had been allowed to practice. They did have to follow strict guidelines set by the department in order to retain their licenses, but the option to practice was still made available to them.

I was willing to follow these guidelines, but the department wouldn't budge. Given my history of repeated episodes of depression, I understood the reluctance to allow me to return to my practice. But now that I had been diagnosed with Bipolar 2 Disorder and receiving the appropriate treatment, I was at a much lower risk of recurrence of my illness. I was hoping that the department would take that into consideration when making their recommendations. Unfortunately, they did not.

It soon became apparent that I would have to go through a long, painful, and expensive legal battle in order to retain my license. I desperately wanted to keep my license, but everyone, including Bobbie, my psychiatrist and my attorney was concerned about how the stress of this tortuous legal skirmish would affect my emotional well-being. With my life, my future at a turning point, I listened to my inner voice, which confirmed what I was now clearly sensing; the door to my career in the practice of medicine was closing. I was at peace with my decision.

I surrendered my license to the medical board, and, in my heart, I surrendered my life to the Will of God.

* * * * *

Now that we had the time, Bobbie and I decided to go on a road trip and explore North Carolina. We started in Raleigh and traveled across the state stopping at various towns along the way. Each locale had its own charm and unique character. But when we arrived in the western part of the state in late November, we fell in love with the Blue Ridge Mountains and knew that this was the place where we wanted to start our new life together. It just felt right.

We moved here in May 2005. During the next year, I was able to reflect and process everything that had happened to me over the last year and before. It was a time of introspection and healing. Although I was no longer practicing medicine, I still wanted to find a way to help other people. It occurred to me that if I shared my story, I could give hope and guidance to people who suffer from or know someone who suffers from mental illness.

It was difficult to write this book because with each chapter, I relived the pain and suffering that I had experienced in my life, but it was also cathartic and integral to my recovery. There is no doubt that a major turning point in my life that started me on the path to wellness occurred when my long-standing diagnosis of major depression was changed to Bipolar 2 Disorder and I received the appropriate treatment. However, from my personal experience, I think that mental illness is not just a matter of brain chemistry gone awry, fixed simply by taking a pill. Medication, though important, is only one piece of the puzzle that has aided in my recovery. There were underlying mental, emotional, physical, and spiritual stressors that also needed to be addressed in order for me to heal.

A variety of methods have helped me and continue to help me in my recovery from my lifetime battle with depression. My decision, after these many years, to love myself unconditionally and accept my imperfections was crucial in healing the wounds of self-hatred and low self-esteem that had scarred my psyche. A cutting-edge form of psychotherapy known as eidetic imagery was also instrumental in healing the emotional trauma caused by the relationship with my mother. Prayer and meditation has deepened my connection to God and, in turn, continues to strengthen me.

Exercise; volunteer work; the love and support of my friends and family, especially Bobbie, are all essential in keeping me healthy. I also take an array of nutritional supplements including vitamins, minerals, and essential fatty acids along with following a diet which is low in processed sugar and refined white flour products, all of which is helpful in improving mood and brain function. In addition, I draw on my knowledge of alternative medicine and use homeopathy, acupuncture, aromatherapy, foot reflexology and Bach flower remedies to help me stay centered and grounded.

To give a balanced perspective, I don't think that it is normal to be happy all the time. Sadness or melancholy is a normal reaction to all the pain and suffering that we are exposed to in this life. One only needs to pick up a newspaper or listen to the news to know that all is not right in this world. The heaviness of heart that we experience from these problems can increase our capacity for compassion and empathy and spur us on to help those in need.

Depression can also sometimes serve as a catalyst for emotional growth. It is a signal that something is wrong and that we need to examine our hearts, minds, and souls to unearth the roots of our discord. These signals should not be ignored because the depression will only continue to fester and have potentially devastating consequences. If the symptoms of depression then begin to have an impact on our ability to function and enjoy life, it is critical that immediate medical intervention be sought.

I used to feel ashamed about having a "mental illness." I considered it to be a sign of weakness. My attitude has changed over the years. Friends, family, and therapists have pointed out to me that I have an inner strength that helped me fight back each time I was knocked down in my lifelong battle with depression. I have finally accepted that fact. It is also my hope that by sharing my life story, other people who suffer from depression, bipolar disorder, or other psychiatric problems will realize that they too have an inner strength that they can call upon to aid them along their path to wellness.

You can contact Dr. Cohen at his Web site

www.alancohenmd.net